Man from the South and Other Stories

ROALD DAHL

Level 6

Retold by Michael Caldon
Series Editors: Andy Hopkins and Jocelyn Potter

Pearson Education Limited
Edinburgh Gate, Harlow,
Essex CM20 2JE, England
and Associated Companies throughout the world.

ISBN 0 582 51223 9

First published in Great Britain by Michael Joseph Ltd 1991
This edition first published by Penguin Books 2002

1 3 5 7 9 10 8 6 4 2

Typeset by Ferdinand Pageworks, London
Set in 11/14pt Bembo
Reproduction by Spectrum Colour, Ipswich
Printed in Spain by Mateu Cromo, S. A. Pinto (Madrid)

Published by Pearson Education Limited in association with
Penguin Books Ltd, both companies being subsidiaries of Pearson Plc

Visit the official Roald Dahl website at
www.roalddahl.com

For a complete list of the titles available in the Penguin Readers series please write to your local
Pearson Education office or to: Marketing Department, Penguin Longman Publishing,
80 Strand, London WC2R 0RL.

Contents

Introduction

It was not until his good strong heart had pumped the last drop of blood from his body that he passed out of this, the best of all possible worlds, into the next.

In this collection of Roald Dahl's short stories, people's lives are changed in some dramatic way and neither they nor the reader can guess what will happen to them until the end. Some of the characters are foolish, some are greedy, some are completely innocent, but they all experience surprise, shock ... or worse. Roald Dahl is the master of the unexpected; the reader has to wait until the final pages of each story to discover the last, terrible twist.

Roald Dahl was born in Britain in 1916 and had an interesting but sometimes unhappy childhood which he described in his book *Boy*. When the Second World War started, he joined the air force. He served first in East Africa and later in the US, where he began to write. The short stories about his time in the air force were published as *Over To You*, and he then produced many more collections of stories, including *Kiss, Kiss* and *Someone Like You*. He also wrote a novel, books about his own life, and his famous children's stories (*James and the Giant Peach*, *Charlie and the Chocolate Factory*, *The BFG* and *Matilda*, for example). Dahl's stories have been translated into numerous languages, and some have been made into films for television and cinema. This is the second book of his stories adapted for Penguin Readers; the first is *Taste and Other Tales*. Roald Dahl is probably one of the best-known and most widely read writers of the twentieth century. He died in November 1990.

Man from the South

It was almost six o'clock, so I thought I'd buy a beer and go out and sit by the swimming pool and have a little evening sun.

I went to the bar and got the beer and carried it outside and wandered down the garden. It was a fine garden and there were plenty of chairs around the pool. There were white tables and huge brightly coloured umbrellas and sunburned men and women sitting around in bathing suits. In the pool itself there were three or four girls and about a dozen boys, all splashing about and making a lot of noise and throwing a large rubber ball at one another.

I stood watching them. The girls were English girls from the hotel. I didn't know about the boys, but they sounded American, and I thought they were probably young sailors from the American ship which had arrived in harbour that morning.

I went over and sat down under a yellow umbrella where there were four empty seats, and I poured my beer and settled back comfortably with a cigarette. It was pleasant to sit and watch the bathers splashing about in the green water.

The American sailors were getting on nicely with the English girls. They'd reached the point where they were diving under the water and pulling the girls up by their legs.

Just then I noticed a small old man walking quickly around the edge of the pool. He was beautifully dressed in a white suit and a cream-coloured hat, and as he walked he was looking at the people and the chairs.

He stopped beside me and smiled. I smiled back.

'Excuse me please, but may I sit here?'

'Certainly,' I said. 'Go ahead.'

He inspected the back of the chair for safety, then he sat down and crossed his legs.

1

'A fine evening,' he said. 'They are all fine evenings here in Jamaica.' I couldn't tell if his accent was Italian or Spanish, but I felt sure he was some sort of a South American. He was old, too, when you looked at him closely. Probably around sixty-eight or seventy.

'Yes,' I said. 'It's wonderful here, isn't it?'

'And who are all these? These are not hotel people.' He was pointing at the bathers in the pool.

'I think they're American sailors,' I told him.

'Of course they are Americans. Who else in the world is going to make as much noise as that? You are not American, no?'

'No,' I said. 'I am not.'

Suddenly one of the young sailors was standing in front of us. He was still wet from the pool and one of the English girls was standing there with him.

'Are these chairs free?' he said.

'Yes,' I answered.

'Mind if I sit down?'

'Go ahead.'

'Thanks,' he said. He had a towel in his hand, and when he sat down he unrolled it and produced a packet of cigarettes and a lighter. He offered the cigarettes to the girl but she refused; then he offered them to me and I took one. The old man said, 'Thank you, no, but I think I will have a cigar.' He took a cigar out of his pocket, then he produced a knife and cut the end off it.

'Here, let me give you a light.' The American boy held up his lighter.

'That will not work in this wind.'

'Sure it'll work. It always works.'

The old man removed the cigar from his mouth, moved his head to one side and looked at the boy.

'Always?' he said slowly.

'Sure, it never fails. Not with me anyway.'

'Well, well. So you say this famous lighter never fails. Is that what you say?'

'Sure,' the boy said. 'That's right.' He was about nineteen or twenty, with pale skin and a rather sharp nose. He was holding the lighter in his hand, ready to turn the little wheel. He said, 'I promise you it never fails.'

'One moment, please.' The hand that held the cigar came up high, as if it were stopping traffic. 'Now just one moment.' He had a curiously soft voice and kept looking at the boy all the time. He smiled. 'Shall we not make a little bet on whether your lighter lights?'

'Sure, I'll bet,' the boy said. 'Why not?'

'You like to bet?'

'Sure, I'll always bet.'

The man paused and examined his cigar, and I must say I didn't much like the way he was behaving. It seemed he was trying to embarrass the boy, and at the same time I had the feeling he was enjoying a private little secret.

He looked up again at the boy and said slowly, 'I like to bet, too. Why don't we have a bet on this thing? A big bet.'

'Now wait a minute,' the boy said. 'I can't do that. But I'll bet you a dollar. I'll even bet you ten, or whatever the money is over here.'

The old man waved his hand again. 'Listen to me. Let's have some fun. We make a bet. Then we go up to my room here in the hotel where there's no wind, and I bet you you cannot light this famous lighter of yours ten times one after another without missing once.'

'I'll bet I can,' the boy said.

'All right. Good. We make a bet, yes?'

'Sure, I'll bet you ten dollars.'

'No, no. I am a rich man and I am a sporting man also. Listen to me. Outside the hotel is my car. It's a very fine car. An American car from your country. Cadillac —'

3

'Now, wait a minute.' The boy leaned back and laughed. 'I can't offer you anything like that. This is crazy.'

'It's not crazy at all. You strike the lighter successfully ten times and the Cadillac is yours. You'd like to have this Cadillac, yes?'

'Sure, I'd like to have a Cadillac.' The boy was still smiling.

'All right. Fine. We make a bet and I offer my Cadillac.'

'What do I offer?'

The old man said, 'I never ask you, my friend, to bet something that you cannot afford. You understand?'

'So what do I bet?'

'I'll make it easy for you, yes?'

'OK. You make it easy.'

'Some small thing you can afford to give away, and if you did lose it you would not feel too bad. Right?'

'Like what?'

'Like, perhaps, the little finger on your left hand.'

'My *what*?' The boy stopped smiling.

'Yes. Why not? You win, you take the car. You lose, I take the finger.'

'I don't understand. How d'you mean, you take the finger?'

'I chop it off.'

'That's crazy. I think I'll just bet ten dollars.'

'Well, well, well,' the old man said. 'I do not understand. You say it lights but you will not bet. Then we forget it, yes?'

The boy sat quite still, staring at the bathers in the pool. Then he remembered that he hadn't lit his cigarette. He put it between his lips, opened the lighter and turned the wheel. It lit and burned with a small, steady, yellow flame, and the way he held his hands meant that the wind didn't get to it at all.

'Could I have a light, too?' I said.

'God, I'm sorry, I forgot you didn't have one.'

He stood up and came over to light my cigarette. There was a silence then, and I could see that the old man had succeeded in disturbing the boy with his ridiculous suggestion. He was sitting there very still, obviously tense. Then he started moving about in his seat, and rubbing his chest and stroking the back of his neck. Finally he placed both hands on his knees and began tapping his fingers against them. Soon he was tapping with one of his feet too.

'Now just let me check I understand,' he said at last. 'You say we go up to your room and if I make this lighter light ten times one time after another I win a Cadillac. If it misses just once then I lose the little finger of my left hand. Is that right?'

'Certainly. That is the bet. But I think you are afraid.'

'What do we do if I lose? Do I have to hold my finger out while you chop it off?'

'Oh, no! That would not be good. And you might refuse to hold it out. What I would do is tie one of your hands to the table before we started, and I would stand there with a knife ready to chop the moment your lighter missed.'

'How old is the Cadillac?'

'How old? It is last year's. Quite a new car. But I see you are not a betting man. Americans never are.'

The boy paused for a moment and he glanced first at the English girl, then at me. 'Yes,' he said suddenly. 'I'll bet you.'

'Good!' The old man clapped his hands together. 'Fine,' he said. 'We will do it now. And you, sir.' He turned to me. 'You would perhaps be good enough to, what do you call it, to – to referee.'

'Well,' I said, 'I think it's a crazy bet. I don't like it very much.'

'Neither do I,' said the English girl. It was the first time she'd spoken. 'I think it's a stupid, ridiculous bet.'

'Are you serious about cutting off this boy's finger if he loses?' I said.

'Certainly I am. Also about giving him my Cadillac if he wins. Come now. We will go to my room. Would you like to put on some clothes first?' he said to the boy.

'No,' the boy answered. 'I'll come like this.' Then he turned to me. 'I'd consider it a favour if you'd come along as a referee.'

'All right,' I said. 'I'll come along but I don't like the bet.'

'You come too,' he said to the girl. 'You come and watch.'

The old man led the way back through the garden to the hotel. He was excited now and that seemed to make him walk with more energy. 'Would you like to see the car first? It's just here.' He took us to a pale-green Cadillac.

'There it is. The green one. You like?'

'That's a nice car,' the boy said.

'All right. Now we will go up and see if you can win her.'

We all went up the stairs and into a large pleasant double bedroom. There was a woman's dress lying across the bottom of one of the beds.

'First,' he said, 'let's have a little drink.'

The drinks were on a small table in the far corner, all ready to be poured, and there was ice and plenty of glasses. He began to pour the drinks, and then he rang the bell and a little later there was a knock at the door and a maid came in.

'Ah!' he said, putting down the bottle and giving her a pound note. 'You will do something for me now please. We are going to play a little game in here and I want you to go off and find for me two – no, three things. I want some nails, I want a hammer, and I want a big knife, a butcher's knife which you can borrow from the kitchen. You can get these, yes?'

'A *butcher's* knife!' The maid opened her eyes wide. 'You mean a real butcher's knife?'

'Yes, of course. Come on now, please. You can find those things surely for me.'

'Yes, sir, I'll try. I'll try to get them.' And she went.

The old man handed round the drinks. We stood there drinking: the boy; the English girl, who watched the boy over the top of her glass all the time; the little old man with the colourless

6

eyes standing there in his elegant white suit, drinking and looking at the girl. I didn't know what to think about it all. The man seemed serious about the bet and he seemed serious about the business of cutting off the finger. But what would we do if the boy lost? Then we'd have to rush him to hospital in the Cadillac that he hadn't won. It would all be a stupid, unnecessary thing in my opinion.

'Before we begin,' the old man said, 'I will present to the – to the referee the key of the car.' He produced the key from his pocket and gave it to me. 'The papers,' he said, 'and the insurance are in the pocket of the car.'

Then the maid came in again. In one hand she carried a butcher's knife, and in the other a hammer and a bag of nails.

'Good! You got them all. Thank you, thank you. Now you can go.' He waited until she had gone, then he put the things on one of the beds and said, 'Now we will prepare ourselves, yes?' The old man moved the little hotel writing-desk away from the wall and removed the writing things. 'And now,' he said, 'a chair.' He picked up a chair and placed it beside the table. 'And now the nails. I must put in the nails.' He fetched the nails and began to hammer them into the top of the table.

We stood there, the boy, the girl and I, watching the man at work. We watched him hammer two nails into the table, about fifteen centimetres apart, allowing a small part of each one to stick up. Then he tested that they were firm with his fingers.

Anyone would think that he had done this before, I told myself. He never hesitated. Table, nails, hammer, knife. He knows exactly what he needs and how to arrange it.

'And now,' he said, 'all we want is some string.' He found some string. 'All right, at last we are ready. Will you please sit here at the table?' he said to the boy.

The boy sat down.

'Now place the left hand between these two nails. The nails

are only so that I can tie your hand in place. All right, good. Now I tie your hand securely to the table – like that.'

He tied the string around the boy's wrist, then several times around the wide part of the hand, then he tied it tightly to the nails. When he finished it was impossible for the boy to pull his hand away. But he could move his fingers.

'Now please, make a fist, all except for the little finger. You must leave the little finger sticking out, lying on the table. Excellent! Excellent! Now we are ready. With your right hand you light the lighter. But one moment, please.'

He hurried over to the bed and picked up the knife. He came back and stood beside the table with the knife in his hand.

'We are all ready?' he said. 'Mr Referee, you must say when to begin.'

'Are you ready?' I asked the boy.

'I'm ready.'

'And you?' to the old man.

'Quite ready,' he said and he lifted the knife up in the air and held it there about sixty centimetres above the boy's finger, ready to cut. The boy watched it, but he didn't react and his mouth didn't move at all. He only raised his eyebrows and frowned.

'All right,' I said. 'Go ahead.'

The boy said, 'Will you please count aloud the number of times I light it.'

'Yes,' I said. 'I'll do that.'

With his thumb he raised the top of his lighter, and again with his thumb he turned the wheel sharply. There appeared a small yellow flame.

'One!' I called.

He didn't blow the flame out; he closed the top of the lighter on it and waited for perhaps five seconds before opening it again. He turned the wheel very strongly and once more there was a small flame.

'Two!'

No one else said anything. The boy kept his eyes on the lighter. The man held the knife up in the air and he too was watching the lighter.

'Three!'

'Four!'

'Five!'

'Six!'

'Seven!' Obviously it was one of those lighters that worked. I watched the thumb closing the top down on to the flame. Then a pause. Then the thumb raising the top once more. The thumb did everything. I took a breath, ready to say eight. The thumb turned the wheel. The little flame appeared.

'Eight!' I said, and as I said it the door opened. We all turned and we saw a woman standing in the doorway, a small black-haired woman, rather old, who stood there for about two seconds then rushed forward, shouting, 'Carlos! Carlos!' She grabbed his wrist, took the knife from him, threw it on the bed, took hold of the man by his jacket and began shaking him with great strength, talking to him fast and loud and fiercely all the time in some Spanish-sounding language. She pulled the old man across the room and pushed him backwards on to one of the beds.

'I am sorry,' the woman said. 'I am so terribly sorry that this should happen.' She spoke almost perfect English. 'It is too bad,' she went on. 'I suppose it is really my fault. For ten minutes I left him alone to go and have my hair washed and I come back and he is doing it again.'

The boy was untying his hand from the table. The English girl and I stood there and said nothing.

'He is a danger to others,' the woman said. 'Where we live at home, he has taken altogether forty-seven fingers from different people, and he has lost eleven cars. In the end they threatened to put him away somewhere. That's why I brought him up here.'

'We were only having a little bet,' whispered the old man.

'I suppose he bet you a car,' the woman said.

'Yes,' the boy answered. 'A Cadillac.'

'He has no car. It's mine. And that makes it worse,' she said. 'He has bet you when he has nothing to bet with. I am ashamed and very sorry about it all.' She seemed a very nice woman.

'Well,' I said, 'then here's the key to your car.' I put it on the table.

'We were only having a little bet,' whispered the old man again.

'He hasn't anything left to bet with,' the woman said. 'He hasn't a thing in the world. Not a thing. In fact I myself won it all from him a long time ago. It was hard work, but I won it all in the end.' She looked up at the boy and she smiled, a slow, sad smile, and she came over and put out a hand to take the key from the table.

I can see it now, that hand of hers; it had only one finger on it, and a thumb.

Beware of the Dog

Down below there was only a vast white sea of clouds. Above there was the sun, and the sun was white like the clouds, because it is never yellow when one looks at it from high in the air.

He was still flying the Spitfire.* His right hand was on the controls. It was quite easy. The machine was flying well. He knew what he was doing.

Everything is fine, he thought. I know my way home. I'll be there in half an hour. When I land I shall switch off my engine and say, 'Help me to get out, will you?' I shall make my voice sound ordinary and natural and none of them will take any notice. Then I shall say, 'Someone help me to get out. I can't do it alone because I've lost one of my legs.' They'll all laugh and think I'm joking and I shall say, 'All right, come and have a look.' Then Yorky will climb up on to the wing and look inside. He'll probably be sick because of all the blood and the mess. I shall laugh and say, 'For God's sake, help me get out.'

He glanced down again at his right leg. There was not much of it left. The bullets had hit him, just above the knee, and now there was nothing but a great mess and a lot of blood. But there was no pain. When he looked down, he felt as if he were seeing something that did not belong to him. It was just a mess which was there; something strange and unusual and rather interesting. It was like finding a dead cat on the sofa.

He still felt fine, and because he still felt fine, he felt excited and unafraid.

I won't even bother to radio for the ambulance, he thought. It isn't necessary. And when I land I'll sit there quite normally and

---

* Spitfire: a British aeroplane, flown in the Second World War.

say, 'Some of you fellows come and help me out, will you, because I've lost one of my legs.' I'll laugh a little while I'm saying it; I'll say it calmly and slowly, and they'll think I'm joking. Then when I get out I'll make my report. Later I'll go up to London. I'll take that bottle of whisky with me and I'll give it to Bluey. We'll sit in her room and drink it. When it's time to go to bed, I'll say, 'Bluey, I've got a surprise for you. I lost a leg today. But I don't mind if you don't. It doesn't even hurt . . .' We'll go everywhere in cars. I always hated walking.

Then he saw the sun shining on the engine cover of his plane. He saw the sun shining on the metal, and he remembered the aeroplane and remembered where he was. He realized that he was no longer feeling good; that he was sick and his head was spinning. His head kept falling forward on to his chest because his neck no longer seemed to have any strength. But he knew that he was flying the Spitfire. Between the fingers of his right hand he could feel the handle of the stick which guided it.

I'm going to faint, he thought. He looked at the controls. Seven thousand metres. To test himself he tried to read the hundreds as well as the thousands. Seven thousand and what? As he looked, he had difficulty reading the dial and he could not even see the needle. He knew then that he must get out; that there was not a second to lose, otherwise he would become unconscious. Quickly he tried to slide back the top, but he didn't have the strength. For a second he took his right hand off the stick and with both hands managed to push the top back. The cold air on his face seemed to help. He had a moment of great clearness. His actions became automatic. That is what happens with a good pilot. He took some deep breaths from his oxygen mask, and as he did so, he looked out over the side. Down below there was only a vast white sea of cloud and he realized that he did not know where he was.

It'll be the English Channel, he thought. I'm sure to fall in the water.

He slowed down, pulled off his mask, undid his safety equipment and pushed the stick hard over to the left. The plane turned smoothly over on to its back and the pilot fell out.

As he fell, he opened his eyes, because he knew that he must not become unconscious before he had opened his parachute. On one side he saw the sun; on the other he saw the whiteness of the clouds, and as he fell, as he turned in the air, the white clouds chased the sun and the sun chased the clouds. Suddenly there was no longer any sun but only a great whiteness. It was so white that sometimes it looked black, and after a while it was either white or black, but mostly it was white. He watched it as it turned from white to black, and then back to white again, and the white stayed for a long time but the black lasted only a few seconds. He seemed to go to sleep during the white periods and to wake up just in time to see the world when it was black.

It was white when he put out a hand and touched something. He took it between his fingers and felt it. For a time he lay there, letting the tips of his fingers play with the thing which they had touched. Then slowly he opened his eyes, looked down at his hand and saw that he was holding something which was white. It was the edge of a sheet. He closed his eyes and opened them again quickly. This time he saw the room. He saw the bed in which he was lying: he saw the grey walls and the door and the green curtains over the window. There were some roses on the table by his bed and beside the roses was a small medicine glass.

This is a hospital, he thought. I am in a hospital. But he could remember nothing. He lay back on his pillow, looking at the ceiling and wondering what had happened. He was staring at the smooth greyness of the ceiling which was so clean and grey, and then suddenly he saw a fly walking upon it. The sight of this fly touched the surface of his brain, and quickly, in that second, he remembered everything. He remembered the plane and he remembered the dial showing seven thousand metres. He remembered jumping out. He remembered his leg.

It seemed all right now. He looked down at the end of the bed, but he could not tell. He put one hand underneath the bedclothes and felt for his knees. He found one of them, but when he felt for the other his hand touched something which was soft and covered in bandages.

Just then the door opened and a nurse came in.

'Hello,' she said. 'So you've woken up at last.'

She was not good-looking, but she was large and clean. She was between thirty and forty and she had fair hair. He did not notice more than that.

'Where am I?'

'You're a lucky fellow. You landed in a wood near the beach. You're in Brighton.* They brought you in two days ago, and now you're better. You look fine.'

'I've lost a leg,' he said.

'That's nothing. We'll get you another one. Now you must go to sleep. The doctor will be coming to see you in about an hour.' She picked up the medicine glass and went out.

But he did not sleep. He wanted to keep his eyes open because he was frightened that if he shut them again everything would go away. He lay looking at the ceiling. The fly was still there. He was still watching it when the nurse opened the door and stood to one side while the doctor came in. He was an Army doctor with some military ribbons from the last war on his chest. He had a cheerful face and kind eyes.

'Well, well,' he said. 'So you've decided to wake up at last. How are you feeling?'

'I feel all right.'

'You'll soon be walking again.' The doctor took his wrist to

* Brighton: a town on the south coast of England.

check his blood pressure. He said, 'Some of the lads from your base were ringing up and asking about you. They wanted to come and see you but I said they'd better wait a day or two. Just lie quiet and rest for a bit. Got something to read?' He glanced at the table with the roses. 'No. Well, the nurse will look after you. She'll get you anything you want.' Then he went out, followed by the nurse.

When they had gone, he lay back and looked at the ceiling again. The fly was still there and as he lay watching it he heard the noise of an aeroplane in the distance. He lay listening to the sound of its engines. It was a long way away. I wonder what it is, he thought. Let me see if I can recognize it. Suddenly he moved his head to one side. Anyone who has been bombed can tell the noise of a German Junkers 88. It is a noise one cannot mistake.

He lay listening to the noise and felt quite certain about what it was. But why was there no alarm and no guns? That German pilot was certainly taking a risk coming near Brighton alone in daylight.

The aeroplane was always far away and soon the noise faded into the distance. Later there was another. This one, too, was far away, but he was sure he recognized the sound. He remembered the noise clearly from air battles he had fought.

He was puzzled. There was a bell on the table by the bed. He reached out his hand and rang it. He heard the noise of footsteps down the corridor. The nurse came in.

'Nurse, what were those aeroplanes?'

'I don't know. I didn't hear them. Probably fighters or bombers. I expect they were returning from France. Why, what's the matter?'

'They were German. I know the sound of the engines. There were two of them. What were they doing over here?'

The nurse came to the side of his bed and began to straighten the sheets.

'You're imagining things. You mustn't worry. Would you like me to get you something to read?'

'No, thank you.'

She brushed back the hair from his forehead with her hand.

'They never come over in daylight any longer. You know that,' she said. 'They were probably British.'

'Nurse.'

'Yes?'

'Could I have a cigarette?'

'Of course you can.'

She went out and came back almost immediately with a packet of cigarettes and some matches. She gave him one, and when he had put it in his mouth she struck a match and lit it.

'If you want me again just ring the bell.' She went out.

Later, he heard the noise of another aircraft. It was far away, but nevertheless he knew that it was a single-engine machine. It was going fast; he could tell that. It wasn't a British aircraft. It didn't sound like an American engine either. They make more noise. He did not know what it was and this worried him greatly. Perhaps I am very ill, he thought. Perhaps I am imagining things. I simply do not know what to think.

That evening the nurse came in with a basin of hot water and began to wash him.

'Well,' she said, 'I hope you don't think that we're being bombed.'

He did not answer. She rubbed some more soap on him and began to wash his chest.

'You're looking fine this evening,' she said. 'They operated on you as soon as you came in. They did a marvellous job. You'll be all right. I've got a brother in the RAF,★ she added. 'Flying bombers.'

★ RAF: (British) Royal Air Force

16

He said, 'I went to school in Brighton.'

She looked up quickly. 'Well, that's fine,' she said. 'I expect you'll know some people in the town.'

'Yes,' he said, 'I know quite a few.'

She had finished washing his chest and arms. Now she turned back the bedclothes so that his left leg was uncovered. She did it in such a way that the rest of his injured leg remained under the sheets. She took his pyjama trousers off and now began to wash his left leg and the rest of his body. This was the first time that he had had a bed-bath and he was embarrassed. She laid a towel under his leg and began washing his foot. She said, 'This soap is awful to use. It's the water. It's so hard.'

He said, 'None of the soap is very good now and, of course, with hard water it's hopeless.' As he said it he remembered something. He remembered the baths which he used to take at school in Brighton. He remembered how the water was so soft that you had to take a shower afterwards to get all the soap off your body. He remembered that sometimes the school doctor used to say that soft water was bad for your teeth.

'In Brighton,' he said, 'the water isn't . . .'

He did not finish the sentence. He had thought of something; something so unbelievable that for a moment he felt like telling the nurse about it and having a good laugh.

She looked up. 'The water isn't what?' she said.

'Nothing,' he answered. 'I was dreaming.'

She wiped the soap off his leg and dried him with a towel.

'It's nice to be washed,' he said. 'I feel better.'

That night he could not sleep. He lay awake thinking of the German aircraft and of the hardness of the water. He could think of nothing else. They were German, he said to himself. I know they were. But it is not possible, because they would not be flying around so low over here in daylight. I know that it is true, and at the same time I know that it is impossible. Perhaps I am ill.

17

Perhaps I am imagining all this. For a long time he lay awake thinking these things, and once he sat up in bed and said aloud, 'I will prove that I am not crazy,' but before he had time to think any more, he was asleep.

He woke just as the first light of day was showing through the gap in the curtains at the window. He remembered the Junkers 88 and the hardness of the water; he remembered the large pleasant nurse and the kind doctor, and now the doubt in his mind began to grow.

He looked around the room. The nurse had taken the roses out the night before. There was nothing except the table with a packet of cigarettes and a box of matches. The room was bare. It was no longer warm or friendly. It was not even comfortable. It was cold and empty and very quiet.

His doubt and fear grew so that he became restless and angry. It was the kind of fear one gets not because one is afraid but because one feels that there is something wrong. He knew that he must do something; that he must find some way of proving to himself that he was either right or wrong, and he looked up and saw again the window and the green curtains. From where he lay, that window was right in front of him, but it was ten metres away. Somehow he must reach it and look out. The idea took hold of him and soon he could think of nothing except the window. But what about his leg? He put his hand underneath the bedclothes and felt the bandages around what remained of his right leg. It seemed all right. It didn't hurt. But it would not be easy.

He sat up. Then he pushed the bedclothes away and put his left leg on the floor. Slowly, carefully, he swung his body over until he had both hands on the floor as well; then he was out of bed, kneeling on the carpet. He looked at what remained of his right leg, wrapped in bandages. It was beginning to hurt. He wanted to lie down on the carpet and do nothing, but he knew that he must go on.

With two arms and one leg, he crawled over towards the window. He would reach forward as far as he could with his arms, then he would jump and slide his left leg along after them. It was painful but he continued to crawl across the floor on two hands and one knee. When he got to the window he reached up, and one at a time he placed both hands on the sill. Slowly he raised himself up until he was standing on his left leg. Then quickly he opened the curtains and looked out.

He saw a small house standing alone beside a narrow lane, and behind it there was a field. In front of the house there was an untidy garden, and there was a green hedge separating the garden from the lane. He was looking at the hedge when he saw the sign. It was just a piece of board nailed to the top of a short pole, and because the hedge had not been cut for a long time the branches had grown out around the sign so that it seemed almost as if it had been placed in the middle of the hedge. There was something written on the board with white paint. He pressed his head against the glass of the window, trying to read what it said. The first letter was a G, he could see that. The second was an A, and the third was an R. One after another he managed to see what the letters were. There were three words, and slowly he spelled the letters out aloud to himself as he managed to read them. G–A–R–D–E A–U C–H–I–E–N, *Garde au chien*.* That is what it said.

He stood there balancing on one leg and holding tightly to the edges of the window sill with his hands, staring at the sign and the letters of the words. For a moment he could think of nothing at all. He stood there looking at the sign, repeating the words to himself. Slowly he began to realize the full meaning of the thing. He looked at the cottage and the field and he looked at the green countryside beyond. 'So this is France,' he said. 'I am in France.'

* *Garde au chien*: *Beware of the dog* in French.

19

Now the pain in his right side was very great. It felt as if someone was hitting the end of his missing leg with a hammer and suddenly the pain became so bad that it affected his head. For a moment he thought he was going to fall. Quickly he knelt down again, crawled back to the bed and got in. He pulled the bedclothes over himself and lay back on the pillow, exhausted. He could not forget the words on the sign.

It was some time before the nurse came in, with a basin of hot water. She said, 'Good morning, how are you today?'

He said, 'Good morning, nurse.'

The pain was still great under the bandages, but he did not wish to tell this woman anything. He looked at her more carefully now. Her hair was very fair. She was tall and big-boned and her face seemed pleasant. But there was something a little nervous about her eyes. They were never still. There was something about her movements also. They were too sharp to go well with the relaxed manner in which she spoke.

She put down the basin, took off his pyjama top and began to wash him.

'Did you sleep well?'

'Yes.'

'Good,' she said. She was washing his chest. 'Someone's coming to see you from the Air Ministry after breakfast,' she went on. 'They want a report. How you got shot down and all that. I won't let him stay long, so don't worry.'

Later she brought him his breakfast but he did not want to eat. He was still feeling weak and sick and he wished only to lie still and think about what had happened. And there was a sentence running through his head. It was a sentence which Johnny, his commanding officer, always repeated to the pilots every day before they went out. He could see Johnny now saying, 'And if they get you, don't forget, only give your name and number. Nothing else. For God's sake, say nothing else.'

'There you are,' she said. 'I've got you an egg. Can you manage all right?'

'Yes.'

'Good. If you want another egg, I might be able to get you one.'

'This is all right.'

'Well, just ring the bell if you want any more.' And she went out.

He had just finished eating when the nurse came in again.

She said, 'Wing Commander Roberts is here. I've told him that he can only stay for a few minutes.' She signalled with her hand and the Wing Commander came in.

'Sorry to bother you like this,' he said.

He was an ordinary RAF officer, dressed in a rather badly fitting uniform. As he spoke he took a printed form and a pencil from his pocket and he pulled up a chair and sat down.

'How are you feeling?'

There was no answer.

'Pity about your leg. I know how you feel. I hear you fought well before they got you.'

The man in the bed was lying quite still, watching the man in the chair.

The man in the chair said, 'Well, let's finish this quickly. I'm afraid you'll have to answer a few questions so that I can fill in my report. Let me see now, first of all, where had you flown from?'

The man in the bed did not move. He looked straight at the Wing Commander and he said, 'My name is Peter Williamson and my number is nine seven two four five seven.'

The Landlady

Billy Weaver had travelled down from London on the slow afternoon train, changing trains on the way, and by the time he got to Bath it was about nine o'clock in the evening. The air was very cold and the wind was like a flat blade of ice on his cheeks.

'Excuse me,' he said, 'but is there a fairly cheap hotel not too far away from here?'

'Try the pub down the road,' a man at the station said, pointing. 'They might take you in. It's about a kilometre along on the other side.'

Billy thanked him and picked up his suitcase and set out to walk to the inn. He had never been to Bath before. He didn't know anyone who lived there, but his boss at the Head Office in London had told him it was a splendid city. 'Find your own accommodation,' he had said, 'and then go along and report to the Local Manager as soon as you've got yourself settled.'

Billy was seventeen years old. He was wearing a new dark blue overcoat, a new brown hat, a new brown suit, and he was feeling fine. He walked briskly down the street. He was trying to do everything briskly these days. All successful businessmen, he had decided, were brisk. The top men at Head Office were brisk all the time. They were amazing.

There were no shops on this wide street, only a line of tall houses on each side, all of them looking the same. They had grand entrances and four or five steps going up to their front doors, and it was obvious that they had been very grand houses indeed. But now, even in the darkness, he could see that the paint was coming off the doors and windows, and that the handsome white exteriors had cracks and patches from lack of repair.

Suddenly, in a downstairs window that was illuminated by a

nearby street lamp, Billy saw a printed notice leaning against the glass in one of the windows. It said BED AND BREAKFAST.

He stopped walking. He moved a bit closer. Green curtains were hanging down on each side of the window. He went right up to it and looked through the glass into the room, and the first thing he saw was a bright fire burning in the fireplace. On the carpet in front of the fire, a pretty little dog was curled up asleep. The room itself, which he could only see in half-darkness, was filled with pleasant furniture. There was a piano and a big sofa and several comfortable armchairs; and in one corner he saw a large parrot in a cage. Animals were usually a good sign in a place like this, Billy told himself, and it looked to him as if it would be a pretty decent house to stay in. Certainly it would be more comfortable than a pub.

On the other hand, a pub would be more friendly than a guesthouse. There would be beer and cards in the evenings, and lots of people to talk to, and it would probably be a lot cheaper, too. He had stayed a couple of nights in a pub once before and had liked it. He had never stayed in any guesthouses and, to be perfectly honest, he was a tiny bit frightened of them. The word 'guesthouse' suggested watery vegetables and greedy landladies.

After hesitating like this in the cold for two or three minutes, Billy decided that he would walk on and look at the pub before making up his mind. He turned to go.

And now a strange thing happened to him. He was just going to step back and turn away from the window when his eye was caught and held in the most peculiar manner by the small notice that was there. BED AND BREAKFAST, it said. BED AND BREAKFAST, BED AND BREAKFAST. Each word was like a large black eye staring at him through the glass, holding him, forcing him to stay where he was and not to walk away from that house, and the next thing he knew, he was actually moving across from the window to the front door, climbing the steps that led to it and reaching for the bell.

23

He pressed it. Far away in a back room he heard it ringing, and then *at once* – it must have been at once because he hadn't even had time to take his finger from the bell-button – the door swung open and a woman was standing there.

She was about forty-five or fifty years old, and the moment she saw him, she gave him a warm welcoming smile.

'*Please* come in,' she said pleasantly. She stepped to one side, holding the door wide open, and Billy found himself automatically starting forward into the house: the force or, more accurately, the desire to follow her was extraordinarily strong.

'I saw the notice in the window,' he said, holding himself back.

'Yes, I know.'

'I was wondering about a room.'

'It's *all* ready for you, my dear,' she said. She had a round pink face and very gentle blue eyes.

'I was on my way to a pub,' Billy told her. 'But I noticed the sign in your window.'

'My dear boy,' she said, 'why don't you come in out of the cold?'

'How much do you charge?'

'Nine pounds a night, including breakfast.'

It was amazingly cheap. It was less than half of what he had been willing to pay.

'If that is too much,' she added, 'then perhaps I can reduce it just a tiny bit. Do you desire an egg for breakfast? Eggs are expensive at the moment. It would cost less without the egg.'

'Nine pounds is fine,' he answered. 'I would like very much to stay here.'

'I knew you would. Do come in.'

She seemed terribly nice. She looked exactly like the mother of one's best schoolfriend welcoming one into the house to stay for the Christmas holidays. Billy took off his hat and stepped inside.

'Just hang it there,' she said, 'and let me help you with your coat.'

There were no other hats or coats in the hall. There were no umbrellas, no walking-sticks – nothing.

'We have it *all* to ourselves,' she said, smiling at him over her shoulder as she led the way upstairs. 'You see, I don't very often have the pleasure of taking a visitor into my little nest.'

The old girl is slightly mad, Billy told himself. But at nine pounds a night, who cares about that? 'I should've thought you'd be simply full of visitors wanting to stay,' he said politely.

'Oh, I am, my dear, I am, of course I am. But the trouble is that I am just a tiny bit careful about whom I choose – if you see what I mean.'

'Ah, yes.'

'But I'm always ready. Everything is always ready day and night in this house just in case an acceptable young gentleman comes along. And it is such a pleasure, my dear, when now and again I open the door and I see someone standing there who is just *exactly* right.' She was halfway up the stairs, and she paused, turned her head and smiled down at him. 'Like you,' she added, and her blue eyes travelled slowly all the way down the length of Billy's body, to his feet, and then up again.

On the first floor she said to him, 'This floor is mine.'

They climbed up more stairs. 'And this one is *all* yours,' she said. 'Here's your room. I do hope you'll like it.' She took him into a small but charming front bedroom, switching on the light as she went in.

'The morning sun comes right in the window, Mr Perkins. It *is* Mr Perkins, isn't it?'

'No,' he said. 'It's Weaver.'

'Mr Weaver. How nice. I've put a hot water bottle between the sheets to warm them, Mr Weaver. And you may light the gas fire at any time if you feel cold.'

'Thank you,' Billy said. 'Thank you very much.' He noticed that the bedclothes had been neatly turned back on one side, all ready for someone to get in.

'I'm so glad you appeared,' she said, looking seriously into his face. 'I was beginning to get worried.'

'That's all right,' Billy answered brightly. 'You mustn't worry about me.' He put his suitcase on the chair and started to open it.

'And what about supper, my dear? Did you manage to get anything to eat before you came here?'

'I'm not hungry, thank you,' he said. 'I think I'll just go to bed as soon as possible because tomorrow I've got to get up rather early and report to the office.'

'Very well, then. I'll leave you now so that you can unpack. But before you go to bed, would you be kind enough to come into the sitting room on the ground floor and sign the book? Everyone has to do that because it's the law, and we don't want to break any laws at *this* stage in the proceedings, do we?' She gave him a little wave of the hand and went quickly out of the room and closed the door.

The fact that his landlady appeared to be slightly crazy didn't worry Billy at all. She was not only harmless – there was no question about that – but she was also quite obviously a kind and generous person. He guessed that she had probably lost a son of her own or something like that, and had never recovered from it.

So a few minutes later, after unpacking and washing his hands, he walked downstairs to the ground floor and entered the sitting room. His landlady wasn't there, but the fire was still burning and the little dog was still sleeping in front of it. The room was wonderfully warm and comfortable. I'm a lucky fellow, he thought, rubbing his hands. This is great.

He found the guest-book lying open on the piano, so he took out his pen and wrote down his name and address. There were only two other names above his on the page and, as one always does, he started to read them. One was a Christopher Mulholland from Cardiff. The other was Gregory W. Temple from Bristol.

That's funny, he thought suddenly. Christopher Mulholland. That name sounds familiar.

Now where had he heard that rather unusual name before? Was he a boy at school? No. Was it one of his sister's numerous young men, perhaps, or a friend of his father's? No, no, it wasn't any of those. He glanced down again at the book. In fact, thinking about it again, he wasn't at all sure that the second name wasn't as familiar to him as the first. 'Gregory Temple?' he said aloud, searching his memory. 'Christopher Mulholland . . .?'

'Such charming boys,' a voice behind him answered, and he turned and saw his landlady walking into the room carrying the tea tray in front of her.

'They sound somehow familiar,' he said.

'They do? How interesting.'

'I'm almost positive I've heard those names before somewhere. Isn't that strange? Maybe it was in the newspapers. They weren't famous in any way, were they? I mean, famous footballers or something like that?'

'Famous,' she said, setting the tray down on the low table in front of the sofa. 'Oh no, I don't think they were famous. But they were extraordinarily handsome, both of them, I can promise you that. They were tall and young and handsome, my dear, just exactly like you.'

Once more, Billy glanced down at the book. 'Look here,' he said, noticing the dates. 'This last entry is over two years old.'

'Is it?'

'Yes, indeed. And Christopher Mulholland's is nearly a year before that – more than *three* years ago.'

'Oh dear,' she said, shaking her head. 'I never would have thought it. How time flies away from us all, doesn't it, Mr Wilkins?'

'It's Weaver,' Billy said. 'W–E–A–V–E–R.'

'Oh, of course it is!' she cried, sitting down on the sofa. 'How silly of me. I do apologize.'

'Do you know something that's extraordinary about all this? Both those names, Mulholland and Temple, I not only seem to remember each one separately but they appear to be connected as well. As if they were both famous for the same sort of thing, if you see what I mean.'

'Well, come over here now, dear, and sit down beside me on the sofa and I'll give you a nice cup of tea and a biscuit before you go to bed.'

Billy watched her as she busied herself with the cups and saucers. He noticed that she had small, white, quickly moving hands, and red fingernails.

'I'm almost positive I saw them in the newspapers,' Billy said. 'I'll think of them in a second. I'm sure I will.'

There is nothing more annoying than a thing like this which remains just outside one's memory. He hated to give up.

'Now wait a minute,' he said. 'Wait just a minute. Mulholland ... Christopher Mulholland ... wasn't *that* the name of the schoolboy who was on a walking tour through the West Country, and then suddenly ...'

'Milk?' she said. 'And sugar?'

'Yes, please. And then suddenly ...?'

'Schoolboy?' she said. 'Oh no, my dear, that can't possibly be right because *my* Mr Mulholland was certainly not a schoolboy when he came to me. He was a university student. Come over here now and sit next to me and warm yourself in front of this lovely fire. Come on. Your tea's all ready for you.'

He crossed the room slowly, and sat down on the edge of the sofa. She placed his teacup on the table in front of him.

'There we are,' she said. 'How nice and comfortable this is, isn't it?'

Billy started drinking his tea. She did the same. For half a minute, neither of them spoke but Billy knew that she was looking at him. Her body was half-turned towards him and he could feel her eyes resting on his face, watching him from over her teacup. Now and again he caught a peculiar smell that seemed to come from her direction. It wasn't unpleasant, and it reminded him – well, he wasn't quite sure what it was. New leather? Or was it the corridors of a hospital?

'Mr Mulholland loved his tea,' she finally said. 'I've never seen anyone in my life drink as much tea as dear, sweet Mr Mulholland.'

'I suppose he left fairly recently,' Billy said.

'Left?' she said. 'But my dear boy, he never left. He's still here. Mr Temple is also here. They're on the third floor, both of them together.'

Billy put down his cup slowly on the table, and stared at his landlady. She smiled back at him and then put out one of her white hands and patted him comfortingly on the knee.

'How old are you, my dear?' she asked.

'Seventeen.'

'Seventeen!' she cried. 'Oh, it's the perfect age! Mr Mulholland was also seventeen. But I think he was a little shorter than you are – in fact I'm sure he was. And his teeth weren't *quite* so white. You have the most beautiful teeth, Mr Weaver. Mr Temple was a little older. He was actually twenty-eight. I wouldn't have guessed it, though, if he hadn't told me. There wasn't a *mark* on his body.'

'A what?' Billy said.

'His skin was *just* like a baby's.'

There was a pause. Billy picked up his teacup, drank some more and then put it down again in its saucer. He waited for her to say something else but she seemed to have fallen into another of her silences. He sat there, looking ahead, biting his lower lip.

'That parrot,' he said at last. 'You know something? It completely fooled me when I looked through the window from the street. I thought it was alive.'

'Sadly, no longer.'

'It's very clever the way it's been stuffed,' he said. 'It doesn't look at all dead. Who did it?'

'I did.'

'*You* did?'

'Of course,' she said. 'And have you met my little Basil as well?'

She nodded towards the dog curled up so comfortably in front of the fire. Billy looked at it. Suddenly he realized that this animal had all the time been as silent and motionless as the parrot. He touched it gently on the top of its back. It was hard and cold but perfectly preserved.

'Good heavens,' he said. 'How very interesting. It must be awfully difficult to do a thing like that.'

'Not at all,' she said. 'I stuff *all* my little pets myself when they die. Will you have another cup of tea?'

'No, thank you,' Billy said. The tea tasted faintly bitter and he didn't really like it.

'You did sign the book, didn't you?'

'Oh, yes.'

'That's good. Because later, if I forget what you were called, then I can always look it up. I still do that every day with Mr Mulholland and Mr . . . Mr . . .'

'Temple,' Billy said. 'Gregory Temple. Excuse me for asking, but haven't there been *any* other guests here except them in the last two or three years?'

Holding her teacup high in one hand, moving her head slightly to the left, she looked at him out of the corners of her eyes and gave him another gentle little smile.

'No, my dear,' she said. 'Only you.'

The Vicar's Pleasure

Mr Boggis was driving the car slowly, leaning back comfortably in the seat with one elbow resting on the open window. How beautiful the countryside is, he thought; how pleasant to see signs of summer again.

He took one hand off the wheel and lit a cigarette. The best thing now, he told himself, would be to drive to the top of the hill. He could see it about a kilometre ahead. And that must be the village at the top of it.

He drove up the hill and stopped the car just before the top of the hill on the outskirts of the village. Then he got out and looked round. Down below, the countryside was spread out in front of him like a green carpet. Perfect. He took a notebook and pencil from his pocket, leaned against the car and allowed his eyes to travel slowly over the landscape.

He could see one medium-sized farmhouse over on the right. There was another larger one beyond it. There was a house surrounded by tall trees that looked rather old, and there were two possible farms away on the left. Five places in all.

Mr Boggis drew a quick sketch in his book showing the position of each so that he'd be able to find them easily when he was down below, then he got back into the car and drove up through the village to the other side of the hill. From there he saw six more possibles – five farms and a big white eighteenth-century house. He studied the house carefully. It looked very grand. That was a pity. He excluded it immediately. There was no point in visiting the rich.

In this area then, there were ten possibles in all. Ten was a nice number, Mr Boggis told himself. Just the right amount for a relaxing afternoon's work. He decided to take the old house with the trees first. It looked dilapidated. The people there probably needed some money. Mr Boggis got back into the car and began driving slowly down the hill.

Apart from the fact that he was at this moment disguised as a vicar, there was nothing very strange about Mr Cyril Boggis. By trade he was a dealer in antique furniture, with his own shop in London. The shop wasn't large, and generally he didn't do a lot of business, but because he always bought cheap, very cheap, and sold at very, very high prices, he managed to make quite a good profit every year. It was said of him by some people that he probably knew as much about French, English and Italian furniture as anyone else in London. He also had surprisingly good taste, and he was quick to recognize and reject an ungraceful design, however genuine the piece might be. His real love was for the work of the great eighteenth-century designers, Chippendale, Robert Adam, Inigo Jones, Hepplewhite, Sheraton and the rest of them.

During the past few years, Mr Boggis had achieved great fame among his friends in the trade by his ability to find unusual and often rare items with amazing regularity. Apparently this man had a source of supply that was never-ending. It seemed that he only had to drive out to it once a week and take what he wanted. Whenever they asked him where he got the things, he would smile and say something about a little secret.

The idea behind Mr Boggis's little secret was a simple one, and it had come to him as a result of something that had happened one Sunday afternoon nearly nine years before, while he was driving in the country.

He had gone out in the morning to visit his old mother and on the way back, in the countryside, his car had broken down, causing the engine to get too hot and the water to boil away. He had got out of the car and walked to the nearest house, a small farm building about fifty metres off the road, and had asked the woman who answered the door if he could have a jug of water.

While he was waiting for her to fetch it, he had glanced in through the door to the living room and seen, not five metres away, something that made him so excited that sweat began to pour down his face. It was a large armchair of a type that he had only seen once before in his life. Each arm of the chair was beautiful and delicate and the back of the chair was decorated with flowers made of wood. The top of each arm was made to look like the head of a duck. Good God, he thought. This chair is late fifteenth century!

He looked further through the door and there was another of them on the other side of the fireplace!

He couldn't be sure, but two chairs like that must be worth thousands of pounds up in London. And how beautiful they were!

When the woman returned, Mr Boggis introduced himself and asked her if she would like to sell her chairs.

Why would she want to sell her chairs? she asked.

No reason at all, except that he might be willing to give her quite a high price.

And how much would he give? They were definitely not for sale, but just for fun, you know, how much would he give?

Thirty-five pounds.

How much?

Thirty-five pounds.

Thirty-five pounds. Well, well, that was very interesting. She'd always thought they were very old. They were very comfortable too. She couldn't possibly do without them. No, they were not for sale, but thank you very much anyway.

They weren't really very old, Mr Boggis told her, and they wouldn't be easy to sell, but he did have a client who rather liked that sort of thing. Maybe he could go up another two pounds – call it thirty-seven. How about that?

They bargained for half an hour, and of course in the end Mr Boggis got the chairs and agreed to pay her something less than a twentieth of their value.

That evening, driving back to London in his old car with the two wonderful chairs in the back, Mr Boggis suddenly had the most brilliant idea.

If there is good furniture in one farmhouse, he said to himself, then why not in others? Why shouldn't he search for it? He could do it on Sundays. In that way, it wouldn't interrupt his work at all. He never knew how to spend his Sundays.

So Mr Boggis bought maps of all the countryside around London, and with a pen he divided each of them up into a series of squares. Each of these squares covered an actual area of ten kilometres by ten, which was about as much territory as he could cope with on a single Sunday. He didn't want the towns and villages. It was the isolated places, the large farmhouses and the old country houses, that he was looking for; and in this way, if he did one square each Sunday, he would gradually visit every farm and every country house around London.

But obviously there was another problem. Country folk are full of suspicion. You can't ring their bells and expect them to show you around their houses, because they won't do it. That way you would never get inside the house. Perhaps it would be best if he didn't let them know he was a dealer at all. He could be the telephone man, the repair man, the gas inspector. He could even be a vicar . . .

From this point, the whole plan began to become more practical. Mr Boggis ordered a large quantity of cards on which the following was printed:

THE REVEREND
CYRIL WINNINGTON BOGGIS
President of the Society
for the Preservation of
Rare Furniture

Every Sunday, he was going to be a nice old vicar spending his

34

holiday travelling around for the 'Society', making a list of the antique furniture that lay hidden in the country homes of England. And who was going to throw him out when they heard that?

Nobody.

And then, when he was inside, if he saw something he really wanted, well – he knew a hundred different ways of dealing with that.

To Mr Boggis's surprise, the scheme worked. In fact, the warmth with which he was received in one house after another was, in the beginning, quite embarrassing, even to him. Sooner or later there had, of course, been some unpleasant incidents, but nine years is more than four hundred Sundays and all that adds up to a lot of houses visited.

Mr Boggis continued to drive, and now it was all farmhouses. The nearest was about a kilometre up the road, set some way back in the fields, and in order to keep his car out of sight, Mr Boggis had to leave it on the road and walk about six hundred metres along a track that led directly into the back yard of the farmhouse. He always parked his large car away from the house he was visiting. He never liked people to see his car until after the deal was completed. A dear old vicar and a large, modern car somehow never seemed quite right together. Also the short walk gave him the opportunity to examine the property closely from the outside. This place, he noticed as he approached, was small and dirty and some of the farm buildings were in a very bad state.

There were three men standing in a close group in a corner of the yard. When these men saw Mr Boggis walking forward in his black suit and vicar's collar, they stopped talking and became absolutely still, three faces turned towards him, watching him with suspicion as he approached.

The oldest of the three was Rummins and he was the owner of the farm.

The tall youth beside him was Bert, Rummins's son.

The short flat-faced man with broad shoulders was Claud.

'Good afternoon,' Mr Boggis said. 'Isn't it a lovely day?'

None of the three men moved. At that moment they were all thinking the same thing – that somehow this vicar, who was certainly not the local fellow, had been sent to look into their business and to report what he found to the government.

'May I ask if you are the owner?' Mr Boggis asked, addressing himself to Rummins.

'What is it you want?'

'I do apologize for troubling you, especially on a Sunday.'

Mr Boggis handed his card and Rummins took it and held it up close to his face.

'And what exactly do you want?'

Mr Boggis explained the aims and ideals of the Society for the Preservation of Rare Furniture.

'We don't have any,' Rummins told him when he had finished. 'You're wasting your time.'

'Now just a minute, sir,' Mr Boggis said, raising a finger. 'The last man who said that to me was an old farmer in Sussex, and when he finally let me into his house, do you know what I found? A dirty-looking old chair in the corner of the kitchen, and it was worth *four hundred pounds*! I showed him how to sell it and he bought himself a new tractor with the money.'

'What are you talking about?' Claud said. 'There's no chair in the world worth four hundred pounds.'

Rummins shifted from one foot to the other. 'Do you mean that you just want to go inside and stand in the middle of the room and look round?'

'Exactly,' Mr Boggis said. 'I just want to look at the furniture to see if you have anything special here, and then I can write about it in our Society magazine.'

'You know what I think?' Rummins said. 'I think you want to buy the stuff yourself. Why else would you take all this trouble?'

'Oh, I only wish I had the money. Of course, if I saw something I liked, and if I could afford it, I might be tempted to make an offer. But, sadly, that rarely happens.'

'Well,' Rummins said, 'I don't suppose there's any harm in you taking a look if that's all you want.'

He led the way to the back door of the farmhouse, and Mr Boggis followed him; so did the son, Bert, and Claud. They went through the kitchen, where the only furniture was a cheap table with a dead chicken lying on it, and they entered a fairly large, extremely dirty living room.

And there it was! Mr Boggis saw it immediately, and he stopped and gave a little cry of shock. Then he stood there for five, ten, fifteen seconds at least, staring like a fool, unable to believe, not daring to believe what he saw before him. It *couldn't* be true, not possibly! But the longer he stared, the more true it began to seem. There it was standing against the wall right in front of him, as real and as solid as the house itself. And who could possibly make a mistake about a thing like that? Yes, it was painted white, but that didn't make the slightest difference. Some fool had done that. The paint could be removed. But good God! Just look at it! And in a place like this!

At this point, Mr Boggis became aware of the three men standing together in a group watching him carefully. They had seen him stop and stare and they must have seen his face turning red, or maybe it was white, but anyway they had seen enough to spoil the whole business if he didn't do something about it quickly. Mr Boggis put one hand over his heart, fell into the nearest chair and breathed heavily.

'What's the matter with you?' Claud asked.

'It's nothing. I'll be all right in a minute. Please — a glass of water. It's my heart.'

Bert fetched him the water, handed it to him, and stayed close beside him, staring down at him.

'I thought maybe you were looking at something,' Rummins said.

'No, no,' Mr Boggis said. 'Oh, no. It's just my heart. It happens every now and again but it goes away quite quickly. I'll be all right in a couple of minutes.'

He *must* have time to think, he told himself. More importantly, he must have time to calm down before he said another word. Go slowly, Boggis. And whatever you do, keep calm. These people may be uneducated, but they are not stupid. And if it is really true – no it *can't* be, it *can't* be true . . .

He was holding one hand over his eyes in a gesture of pain and now, very carefully, he looked through two of his fingers.

The thing was still there. Yes – he had been right the first time! There wasn't the slightest doubt. It was really unbelievable!

What he saw was a piece of furniture that any expert would have given almost anything to have; it was a dealer's dream. Among the most important examples of eighteenth-century English furniture are the three famous pieces known as 'The Chippendale Commodes' and here was the fourth Chippendale Commode! And *he* had found it! He would be rich! He would also be famous! Each of the other three was known throughout the furniture world by a special name. This one would be called The Boggis Commode! Just imagine the faces of the dealers in London when they saw it tomorrow morning! There would be a picture of it in the newspapers, and it would say, 'The very fine Chippendale Commode which was recently discovered by Mr Cyril Boggis, a London dealer . . .' What excitement he was going to cause!

This commode was a most impressive, handsome piece, made in the French style with four elegant legs that raised it about thirty centimetres from the ground. There were six drawers: two long ones in the middle and two shorter ones on each side. The front was beautifully decorated along the top and sides and bottom. The handles, although they were covered with white paint, appeared to be excellent. It was, of course, a rather 'heavy' piece of furniture, but it had been made with such elegant grace that the heaviness was not apparent. It was wonderfully beautiful.

'How are you feeling now?' Mr Boggis heard someone saying.

'Thank you. I'm much better already. It passes quickly. Ah yes. That's better. I'm all right now.'

A little unsteadily, he began to move around the room examining the furniture, one piece at a time, commenting on it briefly. He could see that there was nothing of value apart from the commode.

'A nice table,' he said. 'But it's not old enough to be of much interest. Good comfortable chairs, but quite modern, yes, quite modern. Now this commode' – he walked past and touched it with his fingers – 'worth a few pounds, I'd say, but no more. A rather ugly copy, I'm afraid. Probably nineteenth century. Did you paint it white?'

'Yes,' Rummins said, 'Bert did it.'

'Very wise. It's less ugly in white.'

'That's a strong piece of furniture,' Rummins said. 'Well made, too.'

'Machine-made,' Mr Boggis answered quickly, examining the fine work. He began to walk away but then turned slowly back again. He placed one finger against his chin, laid his head over to one side and appeared deep in thought.

'You know what?' he said, looking at the commode. 'I've just remembered . . . I've been wanting a set of legs like those for a long time. I've got an unusual little table in my own home, one of those low ones people put in front of the sofa and last year, when I moved house, the foolish removal men damaged the legs in the most shocking way. I'm very fond of that table. I always keep my books on it. Now I was just thinking. The legs on this commode might be very suitable. Yes, indeed. They could easily be cut off and fixed on to my table.'

He looked around and saw the three men standing absolutely still, watching him with suspicion, three pairs of eyes, all different but all mistrusting.

Mr Boggis smiled and shook his head. 'But what am I saying? I'm talking as if I owned the piece myself. I do apologize.'

'What you mean to say is, you'd like to buy it,' Rummins said.

'Well ...' Mr Boggis glanced back at the commode. 'I'm not sure. I might ... but on second thoughts ... no ... I think it might be a bit too much trouble. It's not worth it. I'd better leave it.'

'How much were you thinking of offering?' Rummins asked.

'Not much, I'm afraid. You see, this is not a genuine antique. It's just a copy.'

'I'm not so sure about that,' Rummins said. 'It's been in *here* over twenty years. It was old *then*. You can't tell me that thing's new.'

'It's not exactly new, but it's certainly not more than about sixty years old.'

'It's more than that,' Rummins said. 'Bert, where's that bit of paper you once found at the back of one of those drawers? That old bill.'

Mr Boggis opened his mouth, and then quickly shut it again without making a sound. He was beginning to shake with excitement.

When Bert went forward to the commode and pulled out one of the big middle drawers, Mr Boggis noticed the beautiful way in which the drawer slid open. He saw Bert's hand go inside the drawer among a lot of wires and strings. 'You mean this?' Bert lifted out a piece of folded, yellow paper.

'You can't tell me this writing isn't old,' Rummins said, holding the paper out to Mr Boggis, whose arm was shaking as he took it. It said:

> Edward Montagu to Thomas Chippendale
> A large commode of extremely fine wood,
> two very neat long drawers in the middle
> part and two more on each side with handles
> and decoration, all finished to the highest
> standard £87

Mr Boggis was fighting to hide the excitement that was making him feel light-headed. Oh God, it was wonderful! With the original bill, the value had climbed even higher. What would it be now? Twelve thousand pounds? Fourteen? Maybe fifteen or twenty? Who knows?

He threw the paper on the table. 'It's exactly what I told you. A copy. This is simply the bill that the seller – the man who made it and pretended it was an antique – gave to his client. I've seen lots of them.'

'Listen, Reverend,' Rummins said, pointing at him with a thick dirty finger, 'I'm not saying you don't know much about this furniture business, but how can you be so sure it's false when you haven't seen what it looks like under all that paint?'

'Come here,' Mr Boggis said. 'Come over here and I'll show you. Has anyone got a knife?'

Claud gave him a pocket knife and Mr Boggis took it and opened the smallest blade. He scratched off, with extreme care, a small area of white paint from the top of the commode, revealing the old hard wood underneath. He stepped back and said, 'Now, take a look at that!'

It was beautiful – a warm patch of old wood, rich and dark with the true colour of its two hundred years.

'What's wrong with it?' Rummins asked.

'It's been made to look old! Anyone can see that!'

'How can you see that? You tell us.'

'Well, it's difficult to explain. It's a matter of experience. My experience tells me that without the slightest doubt this wood isn't really old.'

The three men moved a little closer to look at the wood. There was an atmosphere of interest now. They were always interested in hearing about new tricks.

'Look closely at the wood. You see that orange colour among the dark red-brown? That shows that it's been made to look older.'

They leaned forward, their noses close to the wood, first Rummins, then Claud, then Bert. The three men continued to stare at the little patch of dark wood.

'Feel it!' Mr Boggis ordered. 'Put your fingers on it! How does it feel, warm or cold?'

'Feels cold,' Rummins said.

'Exactly, my friend! Really old wood has a strangely warm feel to it.'

'This feels normal,' Rummins said, ready to argue.

'No, sir, it's cold. But of course it takes an experienced and sensitive fingertip to be positive. Everything in life, my dear sir, is experience. Watch this.'

From his jacket pocket, Mr Boggis took out a small screwdriver. At the same time, although none of them saw him do it, he also took out a modern little screw which he kept well hidden in his hand. Then he selected one of the screws in the commode – there were four in each handle – and began removing all traces of white paint from its head. When he had done this, he started slowly to unscrew it.

'If this is a genuine eighteenth-century screw,' he was saying, 'it will be irregular and you'll be able to see that it has been hand-cut. But if this is nineteenth-century or later, it will be a mass-produced, machine-made article. We shall see.'

It was not difficult, as he put his hands over the old screw and pulled it out, for Mr Boggis to exchange it for the new one hidden in his hand. This was another little trick of his, and through the years it had proved a most rewarding one. The pockets of his vicar's jacket always contained a quantity of cheap modern screws of various sizes.

'There you are,' he said, handing the modern screw to Rummins. 'Take a look at that. Notice how regular it is? Of course you do. It's just a cheap little screw you yourself could buy today in any shop in the country. My dear friends,' said Mr Boggis, walking towards the door, 'it was so good of you to let me look inside your little home – so kind. I do hope I haven't been a terrible old bore.'

Rummins glanced up from examining the screw. 'You didn't tell us what you were going to offer,' he said.

'Ah,' Mr Boggis said. 'That's quite right. I didn't, did I? Well, to tell you the truth, I think it's a bit too much trouble. I think I'll leave it.'

'How much would you give?'

'Shall we say . . . ten pounds. I think that would be fair.'

'Ten pounds!' Rummins cried. 'Don't be ridiculous, Reverend, *please*!'

'It's worth more than that for firewood!' Claud said.

'All right, my friend – I'll go up as high as fifteen pounds. How's that?'

'Make it fifty,' Rummins said.

A delicious thrill ran all the way down the back of Mr Boggis's legs and then under the bottom of his feet. He had it now. It was his. No question about that. But the habit of buying cheap, as cheaply as possible, was too strong in him now to permit him to give in so easily.

'My dear man,' he whispered softly, 'I only *want* the legs. Possibly I could find some use for the drawers later on, but the rest of it, as your friend rightly said, is firewood, that's all.'

'Make it thirty-five,' Rummins said.

'I *couldn't* sir, I *couldn't*! It's not worth it. And I simply mustn't allow myself to argue like this about a price. It's all wrong. I'll make you one final offer and then I must go. Twenty pounds.'

'I'll take it,' Rummins answered. 'It's yours.'

'Oh dear,' Mr Boggis said. 'I speak before I think. I should never have started this.'

'You can't change your mind now, Vicar. A deal's a deal.'

'Yes, yes, I know.'

'How are you going to take it?'

'Well, let me see. Perhaps if I drove my car up into the yard, you gentlemen would be kind enough to help me load it?'

'In a car? This thing will never go in a car! You'll need a truck for this!'

'I don't think so. Anyway we'll see. My car's on the road. I'll be back in a few minutes. We'll manage it somehow, I'm sure.'

Mr Boggis walked out into the yard and through the gate and then down the long track that led across the field towards the road. He found himself laughing uncontrollably, and there was a feeling inside him as if hundreds of tiny bubbles were rising up from his stomach and bursting in the top of his head. He was finding it difficult to stop himself from running. But vicars never run; they walk slowly. Walk slowly, Boggis. Keep calm, Boggis. There's no hurry now. The commode is yours! Yours for twenty pounds, and it's worth fifteen or twenty thousand! The Boggis Commode! In ten minutes it'll be loaded into your car – it'll go in easily – and you'll be driving back to London and singing all the way!

Back in the farmhouse, Rummins was saying, 'Imagine that old fool giving twenty pounds for a load of old rubbish like this.'

'You did very nicely, Mr Rummins,' Claud told him. 'Do you think he'll pay you?'

'We won't put it in the car till he does.'

'And what will happen if it won't go in the car?' Claud asked.

'You know what I think, Mr Rummins? I think the thing's too big to go in the car. Then he's going to drive off without it and you'll never see him again. Nor the money. He didn't seem very keen on having it, you know.'

Rummins paused to consider this new idea.

Claud went on, 'A vicar never has a big car anyway. Have you ever seen a vicar with a big car, Mr Rummins?'

'I can't say I have.'

'Exactly! And now listen to me. I've got an idea. He told us that it was only the legs he wanted. Right? So if we cut them off quickly right here before he comes back, it will certainly go in the car. All we're doing is saving him the trouble of cutting them off himself when he gets home. How about it, Mr Rummins?'

'It's not such a bad idea,' Rummins said, looking at the commode. 'Come on then, we'll have to hurry. You and Bert carry it out into the yard. Take the drawers out first.'

Within a couple of minutes, Claud and Bert had carried the commode outside and had laid it upside down in the middle of the yard. In the distance, halfway across the field, they could see a small black figure walking along the path towards the road. They paused to watch. There was something rather funny about the way the figure was behaving. Every few seconds it would start to run, then it did a little jump, and once it seemed as if the sound of a cheerful song could be heard from across the field.

'I think he's mad,' Claud said, smiling to himself.

Rummins came over, carrying the tools. Claud took them from him and started work.

'Cut them carefully,' Rummins said. 'Don't forget he's going to use them on another table.'

The wood was hard and very dry, and as Claud worked, a fine red dust fell softly to the ground. One by one, the legs came off, and Bert bent down and arranged them neatly in a row.

Claud stepped back to examine the results of his labour. There was a pause.

'Just let me ask you one question, Mr Rummins,' he said slowly. 'Even now, could *you* put that enormous thing into the back of a car?'

'Not unless it was a van.'

'Correct!' Claud cried. 'And vicars don't have vans, you know. All they've got usually is small cars.'

'The legs are all he wants,' Rummins said. 'If the rest of it won't go in, then he can leave it. He can't complain. He's got the legs.'

'You know very well he's going to start reducing the price if he doesn't get every bit of this into the car. A vicar's just as smart with money as everyone. Especially this old man. So why don't we give him his firewood now and finish it? Where do you keep the axe?'

'That's fair,' Rummins said. 'Bert, go and fetch it.'

Bert went and fetched the axe and gave it to Claud who then, with a long-armed high-swinging action, began fiercely attacking the legless commode. It was hard work, and it took several minutes before he had the whole thing more or less broken in pieces.

'I'll tell you one thing,' he said. 'That was a good carpenter who put this commode together and I don't care what the vicar says.'

'We're just in time!' Rummins called out. 'Here he comes!'

Pig

Once upon a time, in the city of New York, a beautiful baby boy was born, and his joyful parents named him Lexington.

The mother had just returned from hospital carrying Lexington in her arms when she said to her husband, 'Darling, now you must take me out to a most wonderful restaurant for dinner.'

Her husband kissed her and told her that any woman who could have such a beautiful baby as Lexington deserved to go anywhere she wanted. So that evening they both dressed themselves in their best clothes and, leaving little Lexington in the care of a trained nurse who was costing them twenty dollars a day, they went out to the finest and most expensive restaurant in town.

After a wonderful evening, they arrived back at their house at around two o'clock in the morning. The husband paid the taxi driver and then began feeling in his pockets for the key to the front door. After a while, he announced that he must have left it in the pocket of his other suit, and he suggested they ring the bell and get the nurse to come down and let them in. A nurse who was costing them twenty dollars a day must expect to have to get out of bed occasionally in the night, the husband said.

So he rang the bell. They waited. Nothing happened. He rang it again, long and loud. They waited another minute. Then they both stepped back on to the street and shouted the nurse's name up at the nursery window on the third floor, but there was still no answer. The house was dark and silent. The wife began to become frightened. If the nurse couldn't hear the front doorbell, then how did she expect to hear the baby crying?

'You mustn't worry. I'll let you in.' He was feeling rather brave after all he had drunk. He bent down and took off a shoe. Then, holding the shoe by the toe, he threw it hard and straight through the dining-room window on the ground floor.

'There you are,' he said, laughing. He stepped forward and very carefully put a hand through the hole in the glass and undid the lock. Then he raised the window.

'I'll lift you in first, little mother,' he said, and he took his wife around the waist and lifted her off the ground. Then her husband turned her round and began moving her gently through the open window into the dining room. At this moment, a police car came driving silently along the street towards them. It stopped about thirty metres away and three policemen jumped out of the car and started running in the direction of the husband and wife. The policemen were all holding guns.

'Hands up!' the policemen shouted. 'Hands up!' But it was impossible for the husband to obey this order without letting go of his wife. If he had done this, she would either have fallen to the ground or would have been left half in and half out of the house, which is a very uncomfortable position for a woman; so he continued to push her upwards and inwards through the window. The policemen, all of whom had received rewards before for killing robbers, shot at them immediately. Although the policemen were still running, they hit both bodies several times and killed both of them.

So, when he was no more than twelve days old, little Lexington became an orphan.

The news of this killing was brought to all the relatives of the dead couple by newspaper reporters, and the next morning the closest of the relatives got into taxis and left for the house with the broken window. They gathered in the living room and sat around in a circle, smoking cigarettes and talking about what should be done with the baby upstairs, the orphan Lexington.

It soon became clear that none of the relatives wanted

responsibility for the child, and they talked and argued all through the day. Everybody declared an enormous desire to look after him, and would have done so with the greatest of pleasure but their apartment was too small, or they already had one baby and couldn't possibly afford another, or they wouldn't know what to do with the poor little child when they went abroad in the summer, or they were getting old, which would surely be very unfair on the boy. They all knew, of course, that the father had been heavily in debt for a long time and that there would be no money at all to go with the child.

They were still arguing at six the next morning when suddenly, in the middle of it all, an old aunt (her name was Glosspan) arrived from Virginia. Without taking off her hat and coat, without even sitting down, she announced firmly to the gathered relatives that she herself intended to look after the baby boy. She would take full responsibility, she said, for the boy's education – and all the costs – and everyone else could go home. She went upstairs to the nursery and took Lexington and went out of the house with the baby held tightly in her arms. The relatives simply sat, stared, smiled and looked content.

And so the baby, Lexington, left the city of New York when he was thirteen days old and travelled southwards to live with Great Aunt Glosspan in the State of Virginia.

Aunt Glosspan was nearly seventy when she took Lexington to Virginia, but you would never have guessed it. She was as youthful as a woman half her age. She had a small, but still quite beautiful face and two lovely brown eyes. But she was a strange old woman. For the past thirty years she had lived alone in a small cottage high up on the slopes of the Blue Ridge Mountains, several kilometres from the nearest village. She had three cows, some fields for them, some land for growing vegetables, a flower garden and a dozen chickens.

And now she had little Lexington, too.

She was a strict vegetarian and thought that eating animal meat was not only unhealthy and disgusting, but cruel too. She lived on foods like milk, butter, eggs, cheese, vegetables, nuts and fruit, and she was happy to think that no creature would ever be slaughtered for her sake.

She did not know very much about babies but that didn't worry her. At the railway station in New York she bought some things for feeding the baby and a book called *The Care Of Infants*. What more could anyone want? When the train started moving, she fed the baby some milk and laid it down on the seat to sleep. Then she read *The Care Of Infants* from beginning to end.

Strangely there wasn't any problem. Back home in the cottage everything went well. Little Lexington drank his milk and cried and slept exactly as a good baby should, and Aunt Glosspan was filled with joy whenever she looked at him and she kissed him all day long. By the time he was six years old, young Lexington had become a most beautiful boy with long golden hair and deep blue eyes. He was bright and cheerful, and already he was learning to help his old aunt in all sorts of different ways around the farm, collecting the eggs from the chicken house, making butter, and digging up potatoes in the vegetable garden. Soon, Aunt Glosspan told herself, she would have to start thinking about his education.

But she could not bear the thought of sending him away to school. She loved him so much now that it would kill her to be separated from him for long. There was, of course, that village school down in the valley, but it was a horrible-looking place, and if she sent him there, she was sure they would start forcing him to eat meat as soon as he arrived.

'You know what, my darling?' she said to him one day when he was sitting in the kitchen watching her make cheese. 'I'll teach you myself.'

The boy looked at her with his large blue eyes, and gave her a trusting smile. 'That would be nice,' he said.

'And the first thing I should do is to teach you how to cook.'

'I think I would like that, Aunt Glosspan.'

'You're going to have to learn some time,' she said. 'Vegetarians like us don't have nearly so many foods to choose from as ordinary people, and so they must learn to cook doubly well.'

'Aunt Glosspan,' the boy said, 'what do ordinary people eat that we don't?'

'Animals,' she answered with disgust.

'Do you mean live animals?'

'No,' she said. 'Dead ones.'

'Do you mean that when they die they eat them instead of burying them?'

'They don't wait for them to die, dear. They kill them.'

'How do they kill them, Aunt Glosspan?'

'They usually cut their throats with a knife.'

'But what kind of animals?'

'Cows and pigs mostly, and sheep.'

'*Cows!*' the boy cried. 'You mean like our cows?'

'Exactly, my dear.'

'But how do they eat them, Aunt Glosspan?'

'They cut them up into little bits and they cook them. They like the meat best when it's all red and bloody and sticking to the bones. They love to eat cow's flesh with the blood running out of it.'

'Pigs too?'

'They love pigs.'

'Lumps of pig's meat,' the boy said. 'Imagine that. What else do they eat, Aunt Glosspan?'

'Chickens.'

'Chickens? Feathers too?'

'No, dear, not the feathers. Now go outside and play, will you?'

Soon after that, the lessons began. There were five subjects, including reading and writing, but cooking was the most popular with both teacher and pupil. In fact, it soon became very clear that young Lexington was a talented cook. He was clever and quick. In so young a boy, this surprised Aunt Glosspan and she could not quite understand it at all. But she was very proud of him and thought that the child would have a wonderful future.

'How good it is,' she said, 'that I have such a wonderful little fellow to look after me when I'm old.' A couple of years later, she left the kitchen for ever, and put Lexington in charge of all household cooking. The boy was now ten years old, and Aunt Glosspan was nearly eighty. Alone in the kitchen, Lexington immediately began experimenting with dishes of his own invention. There were hundreds of new ideas in his head. Hardly a day went by without some wonderful new dish being placed on the table. There were many delicious inventions. Aunt Glosspan had never tasted food like this in all her life. In the mornings, before lunch, she would go outside the house and sit there in her chair, thinking about the coming meal. She loved to sit there and smell what came through the kitchen window.

Then he would come out, this ten-year-old child, a little smile of pleasure on his face and a big steaming pot of the most wonderful food imaginable in his hands.

'Do you know what you ought to do?' his aunt said to him, eating the food. 'You ought to sit down and write a cookbook.'

He looked at her across the table, eating slowly.

'Why not?' she cried. 'I've taught you how to write and I've taught you how to cook, and now you've only got to put the two things together. You write a cookbook, my darling, and it'll make you famous all over the world.'

'All right,' he said. 'I will.'

And that same day, Lexington began writing the first page of that great book on which he worked for the rest of his life. He called it *Eat Well And Healthily*. Seven years later, by the time he was seventeen, he had recorded over nine thousand different recipes, all of them original, all of them wonderful.

But now, suddenly, his work was interrupted by the death of Aunt Glosspan. She was ill during the night and Lexington found her lying on the bed screaming with pain. She was a terrible sight. The boy wondered what he should do. Finally, to cool her down, he fetched a bucket of water from the river and poured it over her head, but this only made her worse, and the old lady died in an hour.

'This is really too bad,' the poor boy said, pinching her several times to make sure that she was dead. 'And how sudden! Only a few hours ago she seemed in the very best health. She even ate three large portions of my newest mushroom dish and told me how good it was.'

After crying bitterly for several minutes, because he had loved his aunt very much, he carried her outside and buried her in the garden.

The next day, while he was tidying up her things, he found an envelope that was addressed to him in Aunt Glosspan's handwriting. He opened it and took out two fifty-dollar notes and a letter. The letter said:

Darling boy, I know that you have never been down the mountain since you were thirteen days old, but as soon as I die you must put on a pair of shoes and a clean shirt and walk down into the village and find the doctor. Ask the doctor to give you a death certificate. Then take this to my lawyer, a man called Mr Samuel Zuckermann, who lives in New York City and who has a copy of my will. Mr Zuckermann will arrange everything. The money in this envelope is to pay the doctor for the certificate and for the cost of your journey to New York. Mr Zuckermann will give you more money when you get there, and it is my wish that you use it to continue your work on that great book of yours until you are satisfied that it is complete in every way. Your loving aunt,

Glosspan

Lexington, who had always done everything his aunt had told him, put the money in his pocket, put on a pair of shoes and a clean shirt, and went down the mountain to the village where the doctor lived.

'Old Glosspan?' the doctor said. 'Is she dead?'

'Certainly she's dead,' the boy answered. 'If you come home with me now I'll dig her up and you can see for yourself.'

'How deep did you bury her?' the doctor asked.

'Two or three metres down, I think.'

'And how long ago?'

'Oh, about eight hours.'

'Then she's dead,' the doctor announced. 'Here's the certificate.'

Lexington now left for the city of New York to find Mr Samuel Zuckermann. He travelled on foot, and he slept under bushes, and he lived on berries and wild plants, and it took him sixteen days to reach the city.

'What a place this is!' he cried, as he stood staring around him. 'There are no chickens or cows anywhere and none of the women looks like Aunt Glosspan at all.'

Lexington had never seen anyone like Mr Zuckermann before, either.

He was a small man with a large nose, and when he smiled, bits of gold flashed at you from lots of different places inside his mouth. In his office, he shook Lexington warmly by the hand and congratulated him on his aunt's death.

'I suppose you know that your dearly loved aunt was a woman of great wealth?' he said.

'Do you mean the cows and the chickens?'

'I mean five hundred thousand dollars,' Mr Zuckermann said.

'How much?'

'Five hundred thousand dollars, my boy. And she's left it all to you.' Mr Zuckermann leaned back in his chair. 'Of course, I shall have to take 50 per cent for my services,' he said, 'but that still leaves you with two hundred and fifty thousand dollars.'

'I am rich!' Lexington cried. 'This is wonderful! How soon can I have my money?'

'Well,' said Mr Zuckermann, 'luckily for you, I know the people at the city tax office and I'm confident that I'll be able to persuade them to forget about any taxes that your aunt owed.'

'How kind you are,' said Lexington.

'I shall have to give some people a small tip, of course.'

'Whatever you say, Mr Zuckermann.'

'I think a hundred thousand would be enough.'

'But how much does that leave for me?' the youth asked.

'One hundred and fifty thousand. But then you've got the funeral expenses to pay out of that.'

'*Funeral* expenses?'

'You've got to pay the funeral company. Surely you know that?'

'But I buried her myself, Mr Zuckermann, in the field behind the house. I never used a funeral company.'

'Listen,' Mr Zuckermann said patiently. 'You may not know it but there is a law in this State which says that no one can receive any money from a will until the funeral company has been paid.'

'You mean that's a *law*?'

'Certainly it's a law, and a very good law, too. Funerals are one of our country's great traditions. They must be protected at all costs.' Mr Zuckermann himself, together with a group of doctors, controlled a large funeral company in the city. The celebration of death was therefore a deeply religious affair in Mr Zuckermann's opinion. 'You had no right to go out and bury your aunt like that,' he said. 'None at all.'

'I'm very sorry, Mr Zuckermann.'

'It's completely un–American.'

'I'll do whatever you say, Mr Zuckermann. All I want to know is how much I'm going to get in the end, when everything's paid.'

There was a pause.

'Shall we say fifteen thousand?' he suggested, flashing a big gold smile. 'That's a nice figure.'

'Can I take it with me this afternoon?'

'I don't see why not.'

So Mr Zuckermann called his chief clerk and told him to give Lexington fifteen thousand dollars. The youth, who was delighted to be getting anything at all, accepted the money gratefully and put it in his bag. Then he shook Mr Zuckermann warmly by the hand, thanked him for all his help, and went out of the office.

'The whole world is in front of me!' Lexington cried as he went into the street. 'I now have fifteen thousand dollars to help me until my book is ready. After that, of course, I shall have a lot more.' He stood in the street, wondering which way to go. He turned left and began walking slowly down the street, staring at the sights of the city. 'I must have something to eat. I'm so hungry!' he said. The boy had eaten nothing except berries and wild plants for the past two weeks, and now his stomach wanted solid food.

He crossed the street and entered a small restaurant. The place was hot inside, and dark and silent. There was a strong smell of cooking-fat. Lexington seated himself at a corner table and hung his bag on the back of the chair. This, he told himself, is going to be most interesting. In all my seventeen years I have tasted only the cooking of two people, Aunt Glosspan and myself. But now I am going to try the food of a new cook and perhaps, if I am lucky, I might get a few ideas for my book.

A waiter came out of the shadows at the back and stood beside the table. 'Do you want the roast pork and potatoes?' he asked. 'That's all we've got left.'

'Roast what and potatoes?'

The waiter took a dirty handkerchief from his trouser pocket and shook it open. Then he blew his nose loudly. 'Do you want it or don't you?' he said, wiping his nose.

'I don't know what it is,' Lexington answered, 'but I'd love to try it. I'm writing a cookbook and . . .'

'One pork and potatoes!' the waiter shouted, and somewhere in the back of the restaurant, far away in the darkness, a voice answered him.

The waiter disappeared and soon returned carrying a plate on which there lay a thick grey-white piece of something hot. Lexington leaned forward anxiously to smell it.

'But this is absolutely heavenly!' he cried. 'What a smell! It's wonderful!'

The waiter stepped back a little, watching the youth.

'I have never in all my life smelled anything as wonderful as this!' Lexington cried, seizing his knife and fork. 'What is it made of?' But the waiter was moving backwards towards the kitchen. Lexington cut off a small piece of the meat and put it into his mouth, beginning to eat it slowly, his eyes half closed.

'This is wonderful!' he cried. 'It's a fine new flavour! Oh, Glosspan, I wish you were here with me now so that you could taste this dish! Waiter! Come here at once! I want you!'

The waiter was now watching him from the other end of the room.

'If you will come and talk to me, I will give you a present,' Lexington said, waving a hundred-dollar note. 'Please come over here and talk to me.'

The waiter came cautiously back to the table, seized the money and put it quickly into his pocket.

'What can I do for you, my friend?'

'Listen,' Lexington said. 'If you will tell me what this dish is made of, and exactly how it is prepared, I will give you another hundred.'

'I've already told you,' the man said. 'It's pork.'

'And what exactly is pork?'

'Have you never had roast pork before?' the waiter asked, staring.

'Just tell me what it is.'

'It's pig,' the waiter said. 'You just put it in the oven.'

'*Pig!*'

'All pork is pig; didn't you know that?'

'You mean *this* is *pig's* meat?'

'Of course.'

'But ... but ... that's impossible,' the youth said. 'Aunt Glosspan said that meat of any kind was disgusting and horrible, but this is without doubt the most wonderful thing I have ever tasted. How do you explain that?'

'Perhaps your aunt didn't know how to cook it,' the waiter said.

'Is that possible?'

'It certainly is. Especially with pork. Pork has to be very well cooked or you can't eat it.'

'That's it!' Lexington cried. 'That's exactly what must have happened. She cooked it wrong!' He handed the man another hundred-dollar note. 'Lead me to the kitchen,' he said. 'Introduce me to the man who prepared this meat.'

Lexington was at once taken to the kitchen, and there he met the cook, who was an old man with large, unpleasant red patches on his skin.

'This will cost you another hundred,' the waiter said.

Lexington was happy to pay, but this time he gave the money to the cook. 'Now listen to me,' he said. 'I am really rather confused by what the waiter has been telling me. Are you quite sure that the dish I've been eating was prepared from pig's flesh?'

The cook raised his right hand and began scratching his neck.

'Well,' he said, winking at the waiter, 'all I can tell you is that I *think* it was pig's meat.'

'Do you mean you're not sure?'

'One can never be sure.'

'Then what else could it have been?'

'Well,' the cook said, speaking very slowly and still staring at the waiter. 'There's just a chance that it could have been a piece of human flesh.'

'Do you mean – a man?'

'Yes.'

'Good heavens!'

'Or a woman. It could have been either. They both taste the same.'

'Well – now you really surprise me,' the youth said. 'One lives and learns.'

'In fact, we've been getting a lot of it recently from the meat factory in place of pork,' the cook declared.

'Have you really?'

'The trouble is, it's almost impossible to tell which is which. They're both very good.'

'The piece I had just now was wonderful.'

'I'm glad you liked it,' the cook said. 'But to be quite honest, I think that was a bit of pig. In fact, I'm almost sure it was.'

'You are?'

'Yes, I am.'

'In that case we shall have to believe you,' Lexington said. 'So now will you please tell me – and here is another hundred-dollar note for your trouble – will you please tell me how you prepared it?'

The cook, after taking the money, told Lexington how to cook pork, while the youth, not wanting to miss a single word, sat down at the kitchen table and recorded every detail in his notebook.

'Is that all?' he asked when the cook had finished.

'That's all, but you must have a good piece of meat and it must be cut right.'

'Show me how,' said Lexington. 'Kill one now so I can learn.'

'We don't kill pigs in the kitchen,' the cook said. 'The meat you've just eaten came from a slaughterhouse.'

'Then give me the address!'

The cook gave him the address, and Lexington, after thanking them both many times for their kindness, rushed outside and went by taxi to the slaughterhouse.

It was a big brick building, and the air around it smelled sweet and heavy. At the main entrance gates, there was a large notice which said: VISITORS ARE WELCOME AT ANY TIME. Lexington walked through the gates and entered a yard which surrounded the building itself. He then followed some signs (THIS WAY FOR THE GUIDED TOURS) and came to a small hut near the main building (VISITORS' WAITING ROOM). After knocking politely on the door, he went in.

There were six other people in the waiting room. There was a fat mother with her two little boys aged about nine and eleven. There was a bright-eyed young couple and there was a pale woman with long white gloves, looking straight ahead, with her hands folded in front of her. Nobody spoke. Lexington wondered whether they were all writing cookbooks, like himself, but when he put this question to them aloud, he got no answer. They just shook their heads and smiled.

Soon the door opened and a man with a pink face came into the room and said, 'Next, please.' The mother and the two boys got up and went out. About ten minutes later, the same man returned. 'Next, please,' he said again, and the couple stood up and followed him outside.

Two new visitors came in and sat down – a middle-aged husband and a middle-aged wife, the wife carrying a basket.

'Next, please,' said the guide, and the woman with the long gloves got up and left. Several more people came in and took their places on the wooden chairs. Soon the guide returned for the third time, and now it was Lexington's turn to go outside.

'Follow me, please,' the guide said, leading the youth across the yard towards the main building.

'How exciting this is!' Lexington cried.

First they visited a big area at the back of the building where several hundred pigs were wandering around. 'Here's where they start,' the guide said. 'And over there is where they go in.'

'Where?'

'Right there.' The guide pointed to a long wooden shed that stood against the outside wall of the factory. 'This way, please.'

Three men, wearing long rubber boots, were taking a dozen pigs into the shed just as Lexington and the guide arrived, so they all went in together.

'Now,' the guide said, 'watch how they catch them.'

Inside, the shed was simply a bare wooden room with no roof, but there was a metal wire with hooks on it that kept moving slowly along the length of one wall. When it reached the end of the hut, it suddenly changed direction and climbed upwards through the open roof towards the top floor of the main building. The twelve pigs were brought together at the far end of the hut. They stood quietly and looked anxious. One of the men in rubber boots pulled a length of metal chain down from the wall and advanced upon the nearest animal from the back. Then he bent down and quickly put one end of the chain around one of the animal's back legs. The other end he put on a hook on the moving wire as it went by. The wire kept moving and the chain tightened. The pig's leg was pulled up and back, and the pig itself began to be dragged backwards until it reached the end of the hut, where the wire changed direction and went upwards. The creature was suddenly pulled off its feet and was carried up. The pig's cries filled the air.

'Truly interesting,' Lexington said.

The rubber-booted men were busy catching the rest of the

pigs, and one after another the animals were hooked on to the moving wire and carried up through the roof, crying loudly as they went.

At this point, while Lexington was staring upwards at the last pig, a man in rubber boots came up quietly behind him and put one end of a chain around the youth's own leg, hooking the other end of the chain to the moving belt. The next moment, before he had time to realize what was happening, Lexington was pulled off his feet and dragged backwards along the floor of the hut.

'Stop!' he cried. 'Stop everything! My leg is caught!'

But nobody seemed to hear him, and five seconds later the unhappy young man was pulled off the floor and lifted up through the open roof of the hut upside down, hanging like a fish.

'Help!' he shouted. 'Help! There's been a mistake! Stop the engine! Let me down!'

The guide took a cigarette out of his mouth and looked up at the youth hanging from the chain, but he said nothing. The men in rubber boots were already on their way out to collect the next pigs.

'Oh, save me!' Lexington cried. 'Let me down! Please let me down!' But he was now nearing the top floor of the building, where the moving belt entered a large hole in the wall, a kind of doorway without a door; and there, waiting to greet him, in dark-stained rubber clothes, the slaughterer stood.

Lexington saw him only from upside down, and very quickly, but he noticed the expression of absolute peace on the man's face, the cheerfulness in his eyes and the little smile. All these things gave him hope.

'Hi, there!' the man said, smiling.

'Quick! Save me!' Lexington cried.

'With pleasure,' the man said, and taking Lexington gently by one ear with his left hand, he raised his right hand and quickly cut the boy's throat with a knife.

The belt moved on. Lexington went with it. Everything was still upside down and the blood was pouring out of his throat and getting into his eyes, but he could still see a little. He thought he was in a very long room, and at the far end of the room there was a great smoking pot of water, and there were dark figures half hidden in the steam. These figures were dancing round the edge of the pot and they were holding long sticks. The belt seemed to be travelling right over the top of the pot and the pigs seemed to be dropping down one by one into the boiling water and one of the pigs seemed to be wearing long white gloves on its front feet.

Suddenly Lexington started to feel very sleepy, but it was not until his good strong heart had pumped the last drop of blood from his body that he passed out of this, the best of all possible worlds, into the next.

An African Story

In East Africa there was a young man who was a hunter, who loved the plains and the valleys and the cool nights on the slopes of Mount Kilimanjaro. In September 1939 war had begun in Europe and he had travelled over the country to Nairobi and was training to be a pilot with the RAF. He was doing quite well, but after five weeks he got into trouble because he took his plane up and flew off in the direction of Nakuru to look at the wild animals when he should have been practising spins and turns. While he was flying there, he thought he saw some rare animals, became excited and flew down low to get a better view of them. He flew too low and damaged the wing, but he managed to get back to the airfield in Nairobi.

After six weeks, he was allowed to make his first cross-country flight on his own, and he flew off from Nairobi to a little town called Eldoret two thousand metres up in the Highlands. But again he was unlucky; this time he had engine failure on the way, due to water in the fuel tanks. He kept calm and made a beautiful forced landing without damaging his aircraft, not far from a little hut which stood alone on the highland plain with no other building in sight. That is lonely country up there.

He walked over to the hut, and there he found an old man, living alone, with only a small garden of sweet potatoes, some brown chickens and a black cow.

The old man was kind to him. He gave him food and milk and a place to sleep, and the pilot stayed with him for two days and two nights, until a rescue plane from Nairobi found his aircraft, landed beside it, found out what was wrong, went away and came back with clean petrol which enabled him to take off and return.

But during his stay, the old man, who was lonely and had seen no one for many months, was glad of his company and of the opportunity to talk. He talked a lot and the pilot listened. He talked of his lonely life, of the lions that came in the night and of the elephant that lived over the hill in the west, of the heat of the days and of the silence that came with the cold at midnight.

On the second night he talked about himself. He told a long, strange story, and as he told it, it seemed to the pilot that the old man was lifting a great weight off his shoulders by telling it. When he had finished, he said that he had never told that to anyone before, and that he would never tell it to anyone again, but the story was so strange that the pilot wrote it down as soon as he got back to Nairobi. He wrote it in his own words, although he had never written a story before. Of course he made mistakes because he didn't know any of the tricks that writers use, but when he had finished writing he left a rare and powerful story. We found the story in his suitcase two weeks later when we were packing his things after he had been killed in training. The pilot seemed to have had no relatives and because he was my friend, I took the story and looked after it for him. This is what he wrote.

♦

The old man came out of the door into the bright sunshine, and for a moment he leaned on his stick and looked around him. He stood with his head on one side, looking up, listening for the noise which he thought he had heard.

He was small and over seventy years old, although he looked nearer eighty-five because of illness. His face was covered with grey hair, and when he moved his mouth, he moved it only on one side of his face. On his head, indoors or outdoors, he wore a dirty white hat.

He stood quite still in the bright sunshine, his eyes almost closed, listening for the noise.

Yes, there it was again. He looked towards the small wooden hut which stood a hundred metres away in the field. This time there was no doubt about it; the cry of a dog, the high, sharp cry of pain which a dog gives when he is in great danger. Twice more it came and this time the noise was more like a scream. The note was higher and sharper, as if it were torn from some small place inside the body.

The old man turned and walked across the grass towards the wooden hut where Judson lived, pushed open the door and went in.

The small white dog was lying on the floor and Judson was standing over it, his legs apart, his black hair falling all over his long red face, sweating through his dirty white shirt. His mouth hung open in a strange lifeless way, as if his jaw were too heavy for him, and there was spit down the middle of his chin. He stood there looking at the small white dog which was lying on the floor, and with one hand he was slowly twisting his left ear; in the other hand he held a heavy wooden stick.

The old man ignored Judson and went down on his knees beside his dog and gently moved his thin hands over its body. The dog lay still, looking up at him with sad eyes. Judson did not move. He was watching the dog and the man.

Slowly, the old man got up, rising with difficulty, holding the top of his stick with both hands and pulling himself to his feet. He looked around the room. There were dirty bedclothes lying on the floor in the far corner; there was a wooden table made of old boxes, and on it a blue pot. There were chicken feathers and mud on the floor.

The old man saw what he wanted. It was a heavy iron bar standing against the wall near the bedding and he went over to it, thumping the hollow wooden floorboards with his stick as he went. The eyes of the dog followed his movements as he walked with difficulty across the room. The old man changed his stick to his left hand, took the iron bar in his right, came back to the dog and, without pausing, lifted the bar and brought it down hard upon the animal's head. He threw the bar to the ground and looked up at Judson, who was standing there with his legs apart. He went right up to him and began to speak. He spoke very quietly and slowly, with a terrible anger, and as he spoke he moved only one side of his mouth.

'You killed him,' he said. 'You broke his back.'

Then, as the tide of anger rose and gave him strength, he found more words. He looked up and spat them into the face of the tall Judson, who moved back towards the wall.

'You dirty, cruel coward. That was my dog. What right have you got to beat my dog, tell me that. Answer me, you madman. Answer me.'

Judson was slowly rubbing his left hand up and down the front of his shirt and now the whole of his face began to tremble. Without looking up he said, 'He wouldn't stop licking that place on his leg. I couldn't stand the noise it made. You know I can't stand noises like that, licking, licking, licking. I told him to stop but he went on licking. I couldn't stand it any longer, so I beat him.'

The old man did not say anything. For a moment it looked as if he were going to hit this creature. He half raised his arm, dropped it again, spat on the floor, turned round and went out of the door into the sunshine. He went across the grass to where a black cow was standing in the shade of a small tree. The cow was eating, moving its jaws regularly, mechanically, as it watched him walk across the grass from the hut. The old man came and stood beside it, stroking its neck. Then he leaned against its shoulder and scratched its back with the end of his stick. He stood there for a long time, leaning against the cow, scratching it with his stick, and now and then he spoke to it, whispering quiet little words, like one person telling a secret to another.

There was shade under the little tree, and the country around him looked rich and pleasant after the long rains, because the grass grows green up in the Highlands of Kenya, and at this time of the year, after the rains, it is as green and rich as any grass in the world. In the distance stood Mount Kenya with snow on its head, with a thin stream of what looked like white smoke coming from the top where the cold winds made a storm and blew the white powder from the top of the mountain. Down below, on the slopes of that mountain, there were lions and elephants, and sometimes during the night one could hear the roar of the lions as they looked at the moon.

The days passed and Judson went on with his work on the farm in a silent, mechanical way, taking in the corn, digging the potatoes and milking the black cow while the old man stayed indoors away from the fierce African sun. He only went out in the late afternoon when the air began to get cool and sharp, and then he always went over to his black cow and spent an hour with it under the tree. One day, when he came out, he found Judson standing beside the cow, looking at it strangely, standing with one foot in front of the other, gently twisting his ear with his right hand.

'What is it now?' said the old man.

'The cow's making that noise again.'

'She's just chewing the grass,' said the old man. 'Leave her alone.'

Judson said, 'It's the noise. Can't you hear it? It sounds as if she's chewing stones, but she isn't. Listen to her. The noise goes right into my head.'

'Get out,' said the old man. 'Get out of my sight.'

At dawn the old man sat, as he always did, looking out of his window, watching Judson come across from his hut to milk the cow. He saw him coming sleepily across the field, talking to himself as he walked, dragging his feet, leaving long dark green

68

marks across the wet grass, and carrying the petrol can which he used for the milk. The sun was coming up and making long shadows behind the man, the cow and the small tree. The old man saw Judson put the can down and he saw him fetch a box from beside the tree and settle himself on it, ready for the milking. He saw him suddenly kneeling down, feeling under the cow with his hands, and at the same time the old man noticed that the animal had no milk. He saw Judson get up and come walking fast towards the hut. He came and stood under the window where the old man was sitting, and looked up.

'The cow's got no milk,' he said.

The old man leaned through the open window, placing both his hands on the sill. 'You dirty thief! You've stolen it.'

'I didn't take it,' said Judson. 'I've been asleep.'

'You stole it.' The old man was leaning further out of the window, speaking quietly with one side of his mouth. 'I'll beat you for this,' he said.

Judson said, 'Someone stole it in the night. Perhaps it was a native. Or maybe the cow's sick.'

It seemed to the old man that he was telling the truth. 'We'll see,' he said, 'if there's any milk this evening; now, get out of my sight!'

By evening, the cow was full and the old man watched Judson take good thick milk from her.

The next morning she was empty. In the evening she was full. On the third morning she was empty again.

On the third night, the old man went to watch. As soon as it began to get dark, he positioned himself at the open window with an old gun lying on his lap, waiting for the thief who came and milked his cow in the night. At first it was dark and he could not even see the cow, but soon a three-quarter moon came over the hills and it became light, almost as if it were daytime. But it was bitterly cold because the Highlands are two thousand metres up, and the old man pulled his brown blanket closer around his shoulders. He could see the cow well now, just as well as in daylight, and the little tree threw a shadow across the grass, since the moon was behind it.

All through the night, the old man sat there watching the cow, and except when he got up and went back into the room to fetch another blanket, his eyes never left her. The cow stood calmly under the small tree, chewing and staring at the moon.

An hour before dawn she was full. The old man could see it; he had been watching it the whole time, and although he had not seen the movement of the swelling, all the time he had been conscious of the filling as the milk came down. The moon was now low, but the light had not gone. He could see the cow and the little tree and the greenness of the grass around the cow. Suddenly he moved his head quickly. He heard something. Surely that was a noise he heard? Yes, there it was again, right under the window where he was sitting. Quickly he pulled himself up and looked over the sill to the ground.

Then he saw it. A large black snake, a Mamba, nearly three metres long and as thick as a man's arm, was sliding towards the cow. Its small head was raised slightly off the ground and the movement of its body against the wetness made a sound like gas escaping from a jet. He raised his gun to shoot. Almost at once he lowered it again – he didn't know why – and he sat there not moving, watching the Mamba as it approached the cow, listening to the noise it made as it went, watching it come up close to the cow and waiting for it to strike.

But it did not strike. It lifted its head and for a moment let it move gently from side to side; then it raised the front part of its black body into the air under the cow and began to drink from her.

The cow did not move. There was no noise anywhere, and the body of the Mamba curved gracefully up from the ground and hung under the cow. The black snake and the black cow were clearly visible out there in the moonlight. For half an hour the old man watched the Mamba taking the milk of the cow. He saw the gentle movement of the snake's body as it sucked at the liquid until at last there was no milk left. Then the Mamba lowered itself to the ground and slid back through the grass in the direction from which it had come. Again it made a soft noise as it went, and again it passed underneath the window where the old man was sitting, leaving a thin dark mark in the wet grass where it had gone. Then it disappeared behind the hut.

Slowly the moon went down behind the mountain in the distance. Almost at the same time the sun rose in the east and Judson came out of his hut with the petrol can in his hand, walking sleepily towards the cow, dragging his feet in the wet grass as he went. The old man watched him coming and waited. Judson bent down and felt the underneath of the cow, and as he did so, the old man shouted at him. Judson jumped at the sound of the old man's voice.

'It's gone again,' said the old man.

Judson said, 'Yes, the cow's empty.'

'I think,' said the old man slowly, 'that it was a native boy. I was sleeping a bit and only woke up as he was leaving. I couldn't shoot because the cow was in the way. I'll wait for him tonight. I'll get him tonight,' he added.

Judson did not answer. He picked up his can and walked back to his hut.

That night the old man sat up again by the window, watching the cow. For him there was this time a certain pleasure in waiting for what he was going to see. He knew that he would see the Mamba again, but he wanted to be quite sure. And so, when the great black snake slid across the grass towards the cow an hour before sunrise, the old man leaned over the window sill and watched the movements of the Mamba as it approached the cow.

He saw it wait for a moment under the animal's stomach, letting its head move slowly backwards and forwards half a dozen times before it finally raised its body from the ground and started to drink the milk. He saw it drink for half an hour, until there was none left, and he saw it lower its body and slide smoothly back behind the hut from where it had come. And while he watched these things, the old man began laughing quietly with one side of his mouth.

Then the sun rose up behind the hills, and Judson came out of his hut with the petrol can in his hand, but this time he went straight to the window of the hut where the old man was sitting, wrapped up in his blankets.

'What happened?' said Judson.

The old man looked down at him from the window. 'Nothing,' he said. 'Nothing happened. I fell asleep again and the native came and took the milk. Listen, Judson,' he added, 'we have to catch this boy, otherwise you won't have enough milk. We've got to catch him. I can't shoot because he's too clever; the cow's always in the way. You'll have to get him.'

'Me get him? How?'

The old man spoke very slowly. 'I think,' he said, 'I think you must hide beside the cow. That is the only way you can catch him.'

Judson was scratching his head with his left hand.

'Today you will dig a shallow hole beside the cow. If you lie in it and if I cover you over with cut grass, the thief won't notice until he's beside you.'

'He may have a knife,' Judson said.

'No, he won't have a knife. You take your stick. That's all you'll need.'

Judson said, 'Yes, I'll take my stick. When he comes, I'll jump up and beat him with my stick.' Then suddenly he seemed to remember something. 'What about the noise the cow makes when she's chewing?' he said. 'I couldn't stand that noise all night.' He began twisting at his left ear with his hand.

'You'll do as I tell you,' said the old man.

That day Judson dug his hole beside the cow. The cow was tied to the tree so that she could not wander around the field. Then, as evening came and he was preparing to lie down in the hole for the night, the old man came to the door of the house and said, 'Don't do anything until early morning. He won't come until the cow's full. Come in here and wait; it's warmer than your dirty little hut.'

Judson had never been invited into the old man's house before. He followed him in, happy that he would not have to lie all night in the hole. There was a candle burning in the room. It was stuck in the neck of a beer bottle and the bottle was on the table.

'Make some tea,' said the old man. Judson did as he was told. The two of them sat down on a couple of wooden boxes and began to drink. The old man drank his tea hot and made loud sucking noises as he drank. Judson kept blowing on his tea, drinking cautiously and watching the old man over the top of his cup. The old man kept sucking at his tea until suddenly Judson said, 'Stop.' He said it quietly, and as he said it, the corners of his eyes and mouth began to tremble.

'What?' said the old man.

Judson said, 'That noise, that sucking noise you're making.'

The old man put down his cup and looked at the other quietly for a few moments. Then he said, 'How many dogs have you killed, Judson?'

There was no answer.

'I said how many? How many dogs? Judson!' the old man shouted. Then quietly and very slowly, like someone to a child, he said, 'In all your life, how many dogs have you killed?'

Judson said, 'Why should I tell you?' He did not look up.

'I want to know, Judson.' The old man was speaking very gently. 'I'm getting interested in this too. Let's talk about it and make some plans for more fun.'

Judson looked up. A ball of spit rolled down his chin, hung for a moment in the air and fell to the floor.

'I only kill them because of their noise.'

'How often have you done it? I'd love to know how often.'

'Lots of times long ago.'

'How? Tell me how you used to do it. What way did you like best?'

No answer.

'Tell me, Judson. I'd love to know.'

'I don't see why I should tell you. It's a secret.'

'I won't tell. I swear I won't tell.'

'Well, if you promise.' Judson shifted his seat closer and spoke in a whisper. 'Once I waited till one was sleeping, then I got a big stone and dropped it on his head.'

The old man got up and poured himself a cup of tea. 'You didn't kill mine like that.'

'I didn't have time. The noise of its tongue was so bad, the licking. I just had to do it quickly.'

'You didn't even kill him.'

'I stopped the licking.'

The old man went over to the door and looked out. It was dark. The moon had not yet risen, but the night was clear and cold, with many stars. In the east there was a little paleness in the sky, and as he watched, the paleness grew and it changed into brightness. Slowly, the moon rose over the hills. The old man turned and said, 'You'd better get ready. You never know. He might come early tonight.'

Judson got up and the two of them went outside. Judson lay down in the shallow hole beside the cow and the old man covered him with grass, so that only his hand showed above the ground. 'I'll be watching, too,' he said, 'from the window. If I give a shout, jump up and catch him.'

He went back to the hut, went upstairs, wrapped himself in blankets and took up his position by the window. It was early still. The moon was nearly full and it was rising. It shone on the snow on top of Mount Kenya.

After an hour, the old man shouted out of the window, 'Are you still awake, Judson?'

'Yes,' he answered, 'I'm awake.'

'Don't go to sleep,' said the old man. 'Whatever you do, don't go to sleep.'

'The cow's making that noise all the time,' said Judson.

'Good, and I'll shoot you if you get up now,' said the old man.

'You'll shoot me?'

'I said I'll shoot you if you get up now.'

A gentle noise came from where Judson lay, a strange sound as if a child were trying not to cry, and in the middle of it, Judson's voice. 'I've got to move; please let me move. This chewing!'

'If you get up,' said the old man, 'I'll shoot you in the stomach.'

For another hour or so the crying continued, then quite suddenly it stopped.

Just before four o'clock, it began to get very cold and the old man shouted, 'Are you cold out there, Judson? Are you cold?'

'Yes,' came the answer. 'So cold. But I don't mind because the cow's not chewing any more. She's asleep.'

The old man said, 'What are you going to do with the thief when you catch him?'

'I don't know.'

'Will you kill him?'

A pause. 'I don't know. I'll just grab him.'

'I'll watch,' said the old man. 'It should be fun.' He was leaning out of the window with his arms resting on the sill. Then he heard the soft noise under the window, looked out and saw the

75

black Mamba, sliding through the grass towards the cow, going fast and holding its head just a little above the ground as it went.

When the Mamba was five metres away, the old man shouted, 'Here he comes, Judson; here he comes. Go and get him.'

Judson lifted his head quickly and looked up. As he did so he saw the Mamba and the Mamba saw him. There was a second, or perhaps two, when the snake stopped, pulled its head back and raised the front part of its body in the air. Then the stroke. Just a flash of black and a slight thump as it hit him in the chest. Judson screamed, a long high scream which did not rise or fall, but remained constant until gradually it faded into nothingness and there was silence. Now he was standing up, tearing open his shirt, feeling for the place in his chest, crying quietly and breathing hard with his mouth wide open. And the old man sat quietly at the open window, leaning forward and never taking his eyes away from the scene below.

Everything happens very quickly when one is bitten by a snake, by a black Mamba, and almost at once the poison began to work. He fell to the ground, where he lay on his back, rolling around on the grass. He no longer made any noise. It was all very quiet, as if a man of great strength were fighting with someone whom one could not see, and it was as if this invisible person were twisting him and not letting him get up, stretching his arms through the fork of his legs and pushing his knees up under his chin.

Then he began pulling up the grass with his hands and soon after that he lay on his back kicking gently with his legs. But he didn't last very long. He gave a quick shake, twisted his back, then lay on the ground quite still, lying on his stomach with his right knee underneath his chest and his hands stretched out above his head.

Still the old man sat by the window, and even after it was all over, he stayed where he was and did not move. There was a movement in the shadow under the little tree and the Mamba came forward slowly towards the cow. It came forward a little, stopped, raised its head, waited, and slid forward again right under the stomach of the cow. It raised itself into the air and began to drink. The old man sat watching the Mamba taking the milk of the cow, and once again he saw the gentle movement of its body as it sucked out the liquid.

While the snake was still drinking, the old man got up and moved away from the window.

'You can have his share,' he said quietly. 'We don't mind you having his share,' and as he spoke, he glanced back and saw again the black body of the Mamba curving upwards from the ground, joining the underneath of the cow.

'Yes,' he said again, 'we don't mind you having his share.'

The Champion of the World

All day, when not selling petrol, we had been leaning over the table in the office of my petrol station, preparing the raisins. We had a hundred and ninety-six of them to do altogether, and it was nearly evening before we had finished.

'Don't they look wonderful!' Claud cried, rubbing his hands together hard. 'What time is it, Gordon?'

'Just after five.'

Through the window we could see a car arriving at the petrol pumps, with a woman at the wheel and about eight children in the back, eating ice creams.

'We ought to be going soon,' Claud said. 'The plan won't work if we don't arrive before sunset.' He was getting nervous now.

We both went outside, and Claud gave the woman her petrol. When she had gone, he remained standing in the middle of the yard, looking anxiously up at the sun.

'All right,' I said. 'Lock up.'

He went quickly from pump to pump, locking each one.

'You'd better take off that yellow sweater,' he said. 'You'll be shining like a light out there in the moonlight.'

'I'll be all right.'

'You will not,' he said. 'Take it off, Gordon, please. I'll see you in three minutes.'

He disappeared into his hut behind the petrol station, and I went and changed my yellow sweater for a blue one.

When we met again outside, Claud was dressed in a pair of black trousers and a dark-green sweater. On his head he wore a brown cloth cap pulled down low over his eyes.

'What's under there?' I asked, staring at his unusually thick waist.

He pulled up his sweater and showed me two very thin but very large white cotton bags tied neatly and tightly around his waist. 'To carry the stuff,' he said.

'I see.'

'Let's go,' he said.

'I still think we ought to take the car.'

'It's too risky. They'll see it parked.'

'But it's over five kilometres up to that wood.'

'Yes,' he said. 'And I suppose you realize we can get six months in prison if they catch us.'

'You never told me that.'

'Didn't I?'

'I'm not coming,' I said. 'It's not worth it.'

'The walk will be good for you, Gordon. Come on.'

It was a calm, sunny evening, with little clouds hanging motionless in the sky, and the valley was cool and very quiet as the two of us began walking along the grass on the side of the road that ran between the hills towards Oxford.

'Have you got the raisins?' Claud asked.

'They're in my pocket.'

'Good,' he said. 'Wonderful.'

Ten minutes later, we turned left off the main road into a narrow side road with high bushes on either side, and then it was all uphill.

'How many keepers are there?' I asked.

'Three.'

Claud threw away a half-finished cigarette and lit another. 'Don't tell anyone how we've done it, do you understand? Because if anyone heard, every fool in the district would do the same thing, and there wouldn't be a pheasant left.'

'I won't say a word.'

'You ought to be very proud of yourself,' he went on. 'There have been clever men studying this problem for hundreds of years, and not one of them's ever found anything even a quarter as clever as you have. Why didn't you tell me about it before?'

'You never asked for my opinion,' I said.

And that was the truth. In fact, until the day before, Claud had never even offered to discuss with me the subject of poaching. Often, on a summer's evening when work was finished, I had seen him disappearing up the road towards the woods; and sometimes as I watched him through the window of the petrol station, I would wonder exactly what he was going to do, what tricks he was going to practise all alone up there under the trees at night. He seldom came back until very late and he never, absolutely never, brought anything with him on his return. But the following afternoon – I couldn't imagine how he did it – there would always be a pheasant or a rabbit hanging up in the hut behind the petrol station.

This summer he had been particularly active, and during the past couple of months he had been going out four and sometimes five nights a week. But that was not all. It seemed to me that recently his whole attitude to poaching had changed. He was more purposeful about it now, and I suspected that it had become a kind of private war against the famous Mr Victor Hazel himself. Mr Hazel was extremely rich and his property stretched a long way down each side of the valley. He was a brewer, with no charm at all and few good points. He hated all poor people because he himself had once been poor, and he tried to mix with what he believed were the right kind of people. He hunted and gave shooting-parties and every day he drove a big, black Rolls-Royce past the petrol station on his way to and from his factory. As he drove by, we would sometimes see his great, shining face above the wheel.

Anyway, the day before, which was Wednesday, Claud had suddenly said to me, 'I'll be going up to Hazel's woods again tonight. Why don't you come along?'

'Who, me?'

'It's about the last chance this year for pheasants,' he had said. 'The shooting season begins on Saturday, and the birds will be scattered all over the place after that – if there are any left.'

'Why the sudden invitation?' I had asked.

'No special reason, Gordon. No reason at all.'

'I suppose you keep a gun hidden away up there?'

'A gun!' he cried, disgusted. 'Nobody ever *shoots* pheasants, didn't you know that? If you shoot a gun in Hazel's woods, the keepers will hear you.'

'Then how do you do it?'

'Ah,' he said. There was a long pause. Then he said, 'Do you think you could keep your mouth closed if I told you?'

'Certainly.'

'I've never told this to anyone else in my whole life, Gordon.'

'I am greatly honoured,' I said. 'You can trust me completely.'

He turned his head, looking at me with pale eyes. 'I am now going to tell you the three best ways in the world of poaching a pheasant,' he said. 'And, as you're the guest on this little trip, I am going to give you the choice of which one you'd like to use tonight. Now, here's the first big secret.' He paused. 'Pheasants,' he whispered softly, 'are mad about raisins.'

'Raisins?'

'Just ordinary raisins. My father discovered that more than forty years ago. He was a great poacher, Gordon. Possibly the best there's ever been in the history of England. My father studied poaching like a scientist. He really did.'

'I believe you.'

Claud paused and glanced over his shoulder, as if he wanted to make sure there was no one listening. 'Here's how it's done,' he said. 'First, you take a few raisins and you put them in water overnight to make them nice and big and juicy. Then you get a bit of good stiff horsehair and you cut it into small lengths. Then you push one of these lengths through the middle of each raisin, so that there's a small piece sticking out on either side. Do you understand?'

'Yes.'

'So, the pheasant comes along and eats one of these raisins. Right? And you're watching him from behind a tree. So what then?'

'I imagine it sticks in its throat.'

'That's obvious, Gordon. But here's the strange thing. Here's what my father discovered. The moment that happens, the bird never moves his feet again! He becomes absolutely rooted to the spot and you can walk calmly out from the place where you're hiding and pick him up in your hands.'

'I don't believe it.'

'I swear it,' he said. 'You can fire a gun in his ear and he won't even jump. It's just one of those unexplainable little things, but you have to be very clever to discover it.'

He paused and there was a look of pride in his eyes as he thought for a moment of his father, the great inventor.

'So that's method number one,' he said. 'Method number two is even more simple. You take a fishing line. Then you put the raisin on the hook, and you fish for pheasants just as you fish for a fish. You let out the line by about fifty metres, and you lie there on your stomach in the bushes, waiting until a pheasant starts eating. Then you pull him in.'

'What is method number three?' I asked.

'Ah,' he said. 'Number three is the best one. It was the last one my father ever invented before he died. First of all, you dig a little hole in the ground. Then you twist a piece of paper into the shape of a hat and you fit this into the hole, with the hollow end upwards, like a cup. Then you put some glue around the edge. After that, you lay some raisins on the ground leading up to it and drop a few raisins into the paper cup. The old pheasant comes along, and when he gets to the hole he puts his head inside to eat the raisins, and the next thing he knows is that he's got a paper hat stuck over his eyes and he can't see anything. Isn't it wonderful what some people think of, Gordon? Don't you agree? No bird in the world will move if you cover its eyes.'

'Your father was very clever,' I said.

'Then choose which of the three methods you like best, and we'll use it tonight.'

'Yes, but let me ask you something first. I've just had an idea.'

'Keep it,' he said. 'You are talking about a subject you know nothing about.'

'Do you remember that bottle of sleeping pills the doctor gave me last month when I had a bad back?'

'What about them?'

'Is there any reason why they wouldn't work on a pheasant?'

Claud closed his eyes and shook his head.

'Wait,' I said.

'It's not worth discussing,' he said. 'No pheasant in the world is going to swallow those red pills.'

'You're forgetting the raisins,' I said. 'Now listen to this. We take a raisin. Then we put it in water. Then we make a small cut in one side of it. Then we hollow it out a little. Then we open up one of my red pills and pour all the powder into the raisin. Then we get a needle and thread and very carefully we sew up the cut. Now ...'

Out of the corner of my eye, I saw Claud's mouth beginning to open.

'Now,' I said, 'we have a nice, clean-looking raisin with sleeping powder inside it, and that's enough to make the average *man* unconscious; it will easily work on *birds*.'

I paused for ten seconds to allow him time to understand.

'And with this method we could really work with huge numbers. We could prepare twenty raisins if we wanted to, and all

83

we'd have to do is throw them on the ground where the birds feed at sunset and then walk away. Half an hour later, we'd come back and the pills would be beginning to work and the pheasants would be up in the branches by then. They'd feel sleepy and soon every pheasant that had eaten one single raisin would fall over unconscious and fall to the ground. They'd be dropping out of the trees like apples, and we could just walk around picking them up!'

Claud was staring at me.

'And they'd never catch us either. We'd simply walk through the woods, dropping a few raisins here and there as we went, and even if the keepers were watching us, they wouldn't notice anything.'

'Gordon,' he said, 'if this thing works, it will *revolutionize* poaching.'

'I'm glad to hear it.'

'How many pills have you got left?' he asked.

'Forty-nine. There were fifty in the bottle, and I've only used one.'

'Forty-nine's not enough. We want at least two hundred.'

'Are you mad?' I cried.

He walked slowly away and stood by the door with his back to me, looking at the sky. 'Two hundred at least,' he said quietly. 'It's not worth doing it unless we have two hundred.'

What is it now, I wondered. What's he trying to do?

'This is almost the last chance we have before the season starts,' he said.

'I couldn't possibly get any more.'

'You wouldn't want us to come back empty-handed, would you?'

'But why so *many*?'

Claud looked at me. 'Why not?' he said gently. 'Do you have any objections?'

My God, I thought suddenly. He wants to wreck Mr Victor Hazel's opening-day shooting-party.

Mr Hazel's party took place on the first of October every year and it was a very famous event. Gentlemen, some with noble titles and some who were just very rich, came long distances, with their dogs and their wives, and all day long the noise of the shooting rolled across the valley. There were always enough pheasants for everyone; each summer the woods were filled with dozens and dozens of young birds at great expense, but to Mr Victor Hazel it was worth every penny of it. He became, if only for a few hours, a big man in a little world.

'You get us two hundred of those pills,' Claud said, 'and then it'll be worth doing.'

'I can't,' I said. 'Why couldn't we divide one pill among four raisins?'

'But would a quarter of a pill be strong enough for each bird?'

'Work it out for yourself. It's all done by body weight. You'd be giving it about twenty times more than is necessary.'

'Then we'll quarter the amount,' he said, rubbing his hands together. He paused and then thought for a moment. 'We'll have one hundred and ninety-six raisins!'

'Do you realize what that means?' I said. 'They'll take hours to prepare.'

'It doesn't matter!' he cried. 'We'll go tomorrow instead. We'll put the raisins in water overnight and then we'll have all morning and afternoon to get them ready.'

And that was exactly what we did.

Now, twenty-four hours later, we were on our way. We had been walking steadily for about forty minutes, and we were nearing the point where the path curved round to the right and ran along the top of the hill towards the big woods where the pheasants lived. We were about two kilometres away.

'I don't suppose these keepers might be carrying guns?' I asked.

'All keepers carry guns,' Claud said.

I had been afraid of that.

'It's mostly for the foxes,' he added.

'Ah.'

'Of course, they sometimes shoot at a poacher.'

'You're joking.'

'They only do it from behind – when you're running away. They like to shoot you in the legs at about fifty metres.'

'They can't do that!' I cried. 'It's a criminal offence!'

'So is poaching,' Claud said.

We walked on for a while in silence. The sun was low on our right now, and the road was in shadow.

We had reached the top of the hill and now we could see the woods ahead of us, large and dark, with the sun going down behind the trees.

'You'd better let me have those raisins,' Claud said.

I gave him the bag, and he put it gently into his trouser pocket.

'No talking when we're inside,' he said. 'Just follow me and try not to break any branches.'

Five minutes later we were there. The path ran right up to the wood itself and then went round the edge of it for about three hundred metres, with only a few bushes in between. Claud slipped through the bushes on his hands and knees and I followed.

It was cool and dark inside the wood. No sunlight came in at all.

'This is frightening,' I said.

'Sh–h–h!'

Claud was very nervous. He was walking just ahead of me. He kept his head moving all the time and his eyes were looking from side to side, searching for danger. I tried doing the same, but I soon began to imagine a keeper behind every tree, so I gave it up.

Then a patch of sky appeared ahead of us in the roof of the forest, and I knew this must be the feeding grounds.

We were now advancing quickly, running from tree to tree and stopping and waiting and listening and running on again, and then at last we knelt safely behind a big tree, right on the edge of the feeding grounds, and Claud smiled and pointed through the branches at the pheasants.

The place was absolutely full of birds. There must have been two hundred of them at least.

'Do you see what I mean?' Claud whispered.

It was an amazing sight – a poacher's dream. And how close they were! Some of them were not more than ten steps from where we were kneeling. They were brown and so fat that their feathers almost brushed the ground as they walked. I glanced at Claud. His big cow-like face showed his pleasure. The mouth was slightly open, and there was a kind of dream-like look in his eyes as he stared at the pheasants.

There was a long pause. The birds made a strange noise as they moved about among the dead leaves.

'Ah–ha,' Claud said softly a minute later. 'Do you see the keeper?'

'Where?'

'Over on the other side, standing by that big tree. Look carefully.'

'Good heavens!'

'It's all right. He can't see us.'

We knelt close to the ground, watching the keeper. He was a small man with a cap on his head and a gun under his arm. He never moved. He was like a little post standing there.

'Let's go,' I whispered.

The keeper's face was shadowed by his cap, but it seemed to me that he was looking directly at us.

'I'm not staying here,' I said.

'Sh–h–h!' Claud said.

Slowly, never taking his eyes off the keeper, he reached into his pocket and brought out a single raisin. He placed it in his right hand and then quickly threw it high into the air. I watched it as it went over the bushes, and I saw it land within a metre of two birds standing together beside an old tree. Both birds turned their heads at the drop of the raisin. Then one of them jumped over and ate it quickly.

I glanced up at the keeper. He hadn't moved.

Claud threw a second raisin; then a third, and a fourth and a fifth. At this point I saw the keeper turn his head away to look at the woods behind him. Quickly, Claud pulled the paper bag out of his pocket. With a great movement of the arm he threw the whole handful high over the bushes. They fell softly like raindrops on dry leaves. Every pheasant in the place must have heard them fall. There was a noise of wings and a rush to find the raisins. The birds were eating all of them madly.

'Follow me,' Claud whispered. 'And keep down.' He started moving away quickly on his hands and knees, under cover of the bushes.

I went after him, and we went along like this for about a hundred metres.

'Now run!' Claud said.

We got to our feet and ran, and a few minutes later we came out through the bushes into the open safety of the path.

'It went wonderfully,' Claud said, breathing heavily. 'Didn't it go absolutely wonderfully?' His big face was red. 'In another five minutes, it'll be completely dark inside the woods, and that keeper will be going off home to his supper.'

'I think I'll go, too,' I said.

'You're a great poacher,' Claud said. He sat down on the grass bank and lit a cigarette.

The sun had set now and the sky was a pale blue, faintly coloured with yellow. In the wood behind us, the shadows and the spaces between the trees were turning from grey to black.

'How long does a sleeping pill take to work?' Claud asked.

'Look out!' I said. 'There's someone coming.'

The man had appeared silently and suddenly out of the half-darkness, and he was only thirty metres away when I saw him.

'Another keeper,' Claud said.

We both looked at the keeper as he came down the road towards us. He had a gun under his arm, and there was a black dog walking at his feet. He stopped when he was a few steps away, and the dog stopped with him and stayed behind him, watching us through the keeper's legs.

'Good evening,' Claud said in a nice friendly way.

This one was a tall man of about forty with quick eyes and hard, dangerous hands.

'I know you,' he said softly, coming closer. 'I know both of you.'

Claud did not answer this.

'You're from the petrol station, right?' His lips were thin and dry. 'You're Cubbage and Hawes and you're from the petrol station on the main road. Right? Get out.'

Claud sat on the bank, smoking his cigarette and looking at the keeper's feet.

'Go on,' the man said. 'Get out.'

'This is a public road,' Claud said. 'Please go away.'

The keeper moved the gun from his left arm to his right. 'You're waiting,' he said, 'to commit a criminal act. I could have you arrested for that.'

'No, you couldn't,' Claud said.

All this made me rather nervous.

'I've been watching you for some time,' the keeper said, looking at Claud.

'It's getting late,' I said. 'Shall we go on?'

Claud threw away his cigarette and got slowly to his feet. 'All right,' he said. 'Let's go.'

We wandered off down the road, the way we had come, leaving him standing there, and soon the man was out of sight in the half-darkness behind us.

'That's the head keeper,' said Claud. 'His name is Rabbetts.'

'Let's get out of here,' I said.

'Come in here,' Claud said.

There was a gate on our left leading into a field, and we climbed over it and sat down behind the bushes.

'Mr Rabbetts is also due for his supper,' Claud said. 'You mustn't worry about him.'

We sat quietly behind the bushes, waiting for the keeper to walk past us on his way home.

'Here he is,' Claud whispered. 'Don't move.'

The keeper came softly along the road with the dog walking beside him, and we watched them through the bushes as they went by.

'He won't be coming back tonight,' Claud said.

'How do you know that?'

'A keeper never waits for you in a wood if he knows where you live. He goes to your house, hides and watches for you to come back.'

'That's worse.'

'No, it isn't. Not if you put what you've poached somewhere else before you go home. He can't do anything then.'

'What about the other one – the one in the feeding grounds?'

'He's gone, too.'

'You can't be sure of that.'

'I've been watching these men for months, Gordon. Honestly, I know all their habits. There's no danger.'

A few minutes later, I followed Claud back into the wood. It was dark in there now, and very silent, and we moved cautiously forward.

'Here's where we threw the raisins,' Claud said.

I looked through the bushes. The area was illuminated by the moonlight.

'You're quite sure the keeper's gone?'

'I *know* he's gone.'

I could just see Claud's face under his cap, the pale lips, and the large eyes with excitement dancing in each of them.

'Are they asleep?' I asked.

'Yes. In the branches.'

'Where?'

'All around. They don't go far.'

'What do we do next?'

'We stay here and wait. I brought you a light,' he added, and he handed me one of those small pocket torches shaped like a pen. 'You may need it.'

We stood there for a long time, waiting for something to happen.

'I've just had a thought,' I said. 'If a bird can keep its balance on a branch when it's asleep, then surely there's no reason why the pills should make it fall down.'

Claud looked at me quickly.

'It's not dead,' I said. 'It's still only sleeping.'

'It's drugged,' Claud said.

'But that's just a deeper sort of sleep.'

There was a silence.

'We should have tried it first with chickens,' Claud said. 'My father would have done that.'

'Your father was clever,' I said.

At that moment there came a soft thump from the woods.

'Hey!' I said.

'Sh–h–h!'

We stood listening.

Thump! 'There's another!'

It was a heavy sound, as if a small bag of sand had been

dropped from about shoulder height.

Thump! 'They're pheasants!' I cried.

'Wait!'

'I'm sure they're pheasants.'

Thump! Thump!

'You're right!'

We ran back into the wood.

'Where were they?' I asked.

'Over here! Two of them were over here!'

'I thought they were this way.'

'Keep looking!' Claud shouted. 'They can't be far.'

We searched for about another minute.

'Here's one!' he called out.

When I got to him, he was holding a wonderful bird in both hands. We looked at it closely with our torches.

'It's unconscious,' Claud said. 'It's still alive. I can feel its heart.'

Thump! 'There's another,' he cried.

Thump! Thump! 'Two more!'

Thump!

Thump! Thump! Thump!

Thump! Thump! Thump! Thump!

Thump! Thump!

All around us, pheasants were starting to rain down out of the trees. We began to rush around madly in the dark, sweeping the ground with our lights.

Thump! Thump! Thump! This lot fell almost on top of me. I was right under the tree as they came down, and I found all three of them immediately. They were warm, the feathers wonderfully soft in my hands.

'Where shall I put them?' I called out. I was holding them by the legs.

'Lay them here, Gordon! Just pile them there where it's light.'

Claud was standing with the moonlight streaming down all over him and a great bunch of pheasants in each hand. His face was bright, his eyes big and bright and wonderful, and he was staring like a child who has just discovered that the whole world is made of chocolate.

Thump!

Thump! Thump!

'I don't like it,' I said. 'It's too many.'

'It's beautiful!' he cried, and he threw down the birds he was carrying and ran off to look for more.

Thump! Thump! Thump! Thump!

Thump!

It was easy to find them now. There were one or two lying under every tree. I quickly collected six more, three in each hand, and ran back and threw them with the others. Then six more. Then six more after that. And still they kept falling.

Claud was madly happy. He was rushing about under the trees. I could see the beam of his light waving around in the dark, and each time he found a bird, he gave a little cry of pleasure.

Thump! Thump! Thump!

'Mr Victor Hazel ought to hear this!'

'Don't shout,' I said. 'There might be keepers.'

For three or four minutes, the pheasants kept on falling. Then suddenly they stopped.

'Keep searching!' Claud shouted. 'There are a lot more on the ground.'

'Don't you think we ought to stop?'

'No,' he said.

We went on searching. We looked under every tree within a hundred metres of the feeding grounds – north, south, east and west – and I think we found most of them. At the collecting point there was a very big pile of pheasants.

'It's wonderful,' Claud said. 'It's wonderful.' He was staring at them in a kind of dream.

'We'd better just take half a dozen each and get out quickly,' I said.

'I would like to count them, Gordon.'

'There's no time for that.'

'I must count them.'

'No,' I said. 'Come on.'

'One, two, three, four …' He began counting them very carefully, picking up each bird and laying it down gently to one side. The moon was directly above now and everything was illuminated.

'I'm not standing around here like this,' I said. I walked back a few steps and hid myself in the shadows, waiting for him to finish.

'A hundred and seventeen, a hundred and eighteen, a hundred and nineteen, a hundred and twenty!' he cried. 'One hundred and twenty birds! It's an all-time record!'

I did not doubt it for a moment.

'The most my father ever got in one night was fifteen.'

'You're the champion of the world,' I said. 'Are you ready now?'

'One minute,' he answered, and he pulled up his sweater and began to unwind the two big white cotton bags from around his waist. 'Here's yours,' he said, handing one of them to me. 'Fill it up quickly.'

'You don't think that keeper is watching us right now, do you, from behind a tree?'

'There's no chance of that,' Claud said. 'He's down at the petrol station, as I told you, waiting for us both to come home.'

We started loading the pheasants into the bags.

'There'll be a taxi waiting for us in the road,' Claud said.

'What?'

'I always go back in a taxi, Gordon. Didn't you know that? A taxi is impersonal. No one knows who's inside a taxi except the taxi driver. My father taught me that.'

'Which driver?'

'Charlie Kinch. He's glad to help.'

We finished loading the pheasants, and I tried to carry my bag on my shoulder. The bag had about sixty birds in it and it was heavy. Very heavy.

'I can't carry this,' I said. 'We'll have to leave some of them behind.'

'Drag it,' Claud said. 'Just pull it behind you.'

We started off through the black woods, pulling the pheasants behind us.

'We'll never get them all the way back to the village like this,' I said.

'Charlie's never disappointed me yet,' Claud said.

We came to the edge of the woods and looked through the bushes into the road. The taxi was there, not five metres away. Claud said, 'Charlie boy,' very softly, and the old man behind the wheel put his head out into the moonlight and gave us a smile. We slid through the bushes, dragging the bags after us.

'Hello!' Charlie said. 'What's this?'

'Potatoes,' Claud told him. 'Open the door.'

Two minutes later we were safely inside the taxi, driving slowly down the hill towards the village.

It was all over now. Claud was very happy, full of pride and excitement, and he kept leaning forward and tapping Charlie on the shoulder and saying, 'What do you think, Charlie? What do you think about this?' and Charlie kept glancing back at the large full bags lying on the floor between us and saying, 'How did you do it?'

'There's a dozen of them for you, Charlie,' Claud said.

Charlie said, 'I think pheasants are going to be a bit scarce up at Mr Hazel's opening-day shooting-party this year,' and Claud said, 'I imagine they are, Charlie. I imagine they are.'

'What are you going to do with a hundred and twenty pheasants?' I asked.

'Put them in the freezer at the petrol station,' Claud said.

'Not tonight, I hope.'

'No, Gordon, not tonight. We leave them at Bessie's house tonight.'

'Bessie who?'

'Bessie Organ.'

'Bessie Organ!' I was absolutely amazed. Mrs Organ was the wife of the local vicar, Jack Organ.

'Bessie always delivers my birds. Didn't you know that?'

'I don't know anything,' I said.

'Bessie's a clever girl,' Charlie said.

We were driving through the village now and the street lamps were still on and the men were wandering home from the pub.

'The vicar loves a roast pheasant,' Claud said.

The taxi turned left and went in through the gates of the vicar's house. There were no lights on there, and nobody met us. Claud and I put the pheasants in the hut behind the house, and then we said goodbye to Charlie Kinch and walked back in the moonlight to the petrol station. I don't know whether or not Mr Rabbetts was watching us as we went in.

'Here she comes,' Claud said to me the next morning.

'Who?'

'Bessie – Bessie Organ.' He spoke the name proudly, as if he were a general referring to his bravest officer. 'Down there,' he said, pointing.

Far away down the road, I could see a small female figure advancing towards us.

'What's she pushing?' I asked.

96

'There's only one safe way of delivering pheasants,' he announced, 'and that's under a baby.'

'Yes,' I said. 'Of course.'

'That'll be young Christopher Organ in the pram, aged one and a half years. He's a lovely child, Gordon.'

I could just see the small face of a baby sitting up high in the pram.

'There are sixty or seventy pheasants at least under that little lad,' Claud said happily. 'Just imagine that.'

'You can't fit sixty or seventy pheasants into a pram,' I said.

'You can if it's got a good, deep space underneath it, and if you pack them in tightly, right up to the top. All you need is a sheet. You'd be surprised how little room a pheasant takes up when it's asleep.'

We waited by the pumps for Bessie Organ to arrive. It was one of those warm, windless September mornings, with a darkening sky and a smell of thunder in the air.

'Right through the village,' Claud said. 'Good old Bessie.'

'She seems in rather a hurry to me.'

Claud lit a new cigarette. 'Bessie is never in a hurry,' he said.

'She certainly isn't walking slowly,' I told him. 'Look.'

He looked at her through the smoke of his cigarette. Then he took the cigarette out of his mouth and looked again.

'Well?' I said.

'She does seem to be going rather quickly, doesn't she?' he said carefully.

'She's going *very* quickly.'

There was a pause. Claud was beginning to stare very hard at the approaching woman. 'Perhaps she doesn't want to get caught in the rain, Gordon. She thinks it's going to rain, and she doesn't want the baby to get wet.'

'She's *running*,' I cried. 'Look!' Bessie had suddenly started to run at top speed.

Claud stood very still, watching the woman; and in the silence that followed, I thought I could hear a baby screaming.

'There's something wrong with that baby,' I said. 'Listen.'

At this point, Bessie was about two hundred metres away from us, but was approaching fast.

'Can you hear him now?' I said. 'He's screaming his head off.'

The small, high voice in the distance was growing louder every second.

'Perhaps the baby's ill. There are a thousand and one things that can happen to little babies like that,' Claud said.

'Of course.'

'Whatever it is,' he continued, 'I wish she'd stop running.'

A long lorry loaded with bricks came up beside Bessie, and the driver slowed down and put his head out of the window to stare. Bessie ran on, and she was so close now that I could see her big red face, with the mouth wide open, breathing heavily.

Suddenly, out of the pram, straight up into the air, flew an enormous pheasant.

Claud let out a cry of terror.

The fool in the lorry going along beside Bessie roared with laughter. The pheasant flew around sleepily for a few seconds, then it lost height and landed in the grass by the side of the road. Bessie kept on running.

Then a second pheasant flew up out of the pram.

Then a third and a fourth. Then a fifth.

'My God!' I said. 'It's the pills! They've stopped working!'

Bessie covered the last fifty metres at a great speed, and she came running up to the petrol station with birds flying up out of the pram in all directions.

'What's going on?' she cried.

'Go round the back!' I shouted.

But she stopped beside the first pump in the line, and before we could reach her she had seized the screaming baby in her arms and dragged him out of the pram.

'No! No!' Claud cried, running towards her. 'Don't lift the baby! Put him back! Hold down the sheet!' But she wasn't even listening, and as the weight of the child was suddenly lifted away, a great cloud of pheasants rose up out of the pram – forty or fifty of them at least – and the whole sky above us was filled with huge brown birds beating their wings madly to gain height.

Claud and I started running up and down, waving our arms to frighten them away. 'Go away!' we shouted. 'Shoo! Go away!' But they were too drugged still to take any notice of us, and within half a minute they had come down again and settled themselves all over the front of my petrol station. The place was covered with them. They sat wing to wing along the edges of the roof and a dozen, at least, were sitting on the office window sill. Others were sliding about on top of my second-hand cars. One bird with a fine tail was sitting on top of a petrol pump, and quite a number sat at our feet, shaking their feathers.

Across the road, a line of cars had already started forming behind the brick lorry, and people were opening their doors and getting out and beginning to cross over to have a closer look. I glanced at my watch. It was twenty to nine. At any moment now, I thought, a large black car is going to come along the road from the direction of the village, and the car will be a Rolls-Royce, and the face behind the wheel will be the great shiny brewer's face of Mr Victor Hazel.

'They attacked him!' Bessie was shouting, holding the screaming baby to her chest.

'You go on home, Bessie,' Claud said, white in the face.

'Lock up,' I said. 'Put out the sign. We've gone for the day.'

ACTIVITIES

'Man from the South' and 'Beware of the Dog'

Before you read

1 Discuss these questions.

   a What do people commonly bet on? Why do they continue betting even when they lose?

   b One of these stories is about a British pilot in the Second World War (1939–45). His plane has been hit and he has been injured. How do you think he feels? What decisions must he make?

2 Find these words in your dictionary. They are used in these stories. Put them in the sentences below.

   beware   chop   cigar   maid   mask   parachute   sill
   Wing Commander

   a It was time to open my . . . . . .

   b I only smoke . . . . . .

   c The . . . . . gave us our final orders.

   d She climbed out on to the window . . . . . .

   e . . . . . of falling rocks!

   f Please ask the . . . . . to clean our room now.

   g We had to wear . . . . . to protect us from poisonous gases.

   h First, ... the meat into small pieces.

After you read

3 In what way are these objects important to the plot of 'Man from the South'?

   a a cigarette lighter   c a butcher's knife

   b a Cadillac   d a piece of string

4 Discuss why the American boy agreed to the older man's bet. Would you have agreed? Why (not)?

5 Work with a partner. Have this conversation.

   Student A: You are another doctor in 'Beware of the Dog', pretending to be British. Ask the pilot questions. Find out if he knows where he is. Try to discover secret information.

Student B: You are the pilot. Persuade the doctor that you believe you are in Brighton. Try not to tell him anything else.

'The Landlady' and 'The Vicar's Pleasure'

Before you read

6   Find the word *vicar* in your dictionary. What do you think the main responsibilities are of
   a a vicar?
   b the landlady of a guesthouse?
7   Answer the questions. Find the words in *italics* in your dictionary.
   a What are these used for?
       an *axe*   a *commode*   a *sketch*   a *tray*
   b Who is given the title *Reverend*?
   c Explain these phrases in your own words.
       a *brisk* walk   a *dilapidated* building
       an *illuminated* football ground

After you read

8   Answer these questions about 'The Landlady'.
   a Why is Billy Weaver visiting Bath?
   b Why does he decide to stay in the guesthouse instead of a pub?
   c Why does Billy know the names of the landlady's previous guests?
   d Why is it important to the landlady that Billy drinks his tea?
9   Explain why, in 'The Vicar's Pleasure',
   a Mr Boggis runs, jumps and sings as he crosses the field to his car.
   b Rummins, Bert and Claud break the commode into little pieces.
10 How do the landlady and Mr Boggis (usually) succeed in their aims? Discuss why people trust them.

'Pig' and 'An African Story'

Before you read

11 The main characters in both these stories live far away from towns

and other people. Discuss the advantages and disadvantages of living such a quiet life.

12 Find the words in *italics* in your dictionary.

   a Show your understanding of these words by acting them out.

      lick   thump   slaughter   wink

   b Which of the words below is a word for

     a document? a building? a person?

     shed   vegetarian   will

After you read

13 Are these statements about 'Pig' true or false? Correct the false ones.

   a Lexington's parents are shot because they are burglars.

   b His relatives all want to bring him up.

   c In Aunt Glosspan's home, he never eats meat.

   d He is a very talented cook.

   e If he had remained vegetarian, he wouldn't have died.

14 Lexington is a very innocent young man.

   a Give two examples of the ways in which people use this quality to get money out of him.

   b Discuss how much money Lexington probably had with him when he died.

15 Discuss these questions about Judson in 'An African Story'.

   a Was he cruel or mad? What evidence is there for this?

   b Why did the old man want to kill him?

   c Why didn't the old man just shoot him?

16 Dahl paints a clear picture of the area of the Kenyan Highlands where the old man lives. Describe the old man's world in your own words.

'The Champion of the World'

Before you read

17 This story is about people who kill animals for food and for pleasure. Explain your views on hunting as a sport.

18 Find these words in your dictionary.

brewer   keeper   pheasant   poach   pram   raisin

Which word describes

a a bird you can eat?

b a kind of dried fruit?

c illegal hunting?

d a baby carriage?

e a person who makes beer?

f a person who guards animals?

After you read

19 As Gordon and Claud set out on their poaching expedition, who says these words? What are they talking about?

a 'Take it off, please.'

b 'To carry the stuff.'

c 'It's too risky.'

d 'They're in my pocket.'

e 'I won't say a word.'

20 Discuss Claud's usual methods of poaching pheasants. Which would be the most difficult? Why?

21 Work in groups of four. Take the roles of Claud, Gordon, Bessie and Mr Hazel. Imagine their conversation after the end of the story and act it out.

Writing

22 Carlos's wife in 'Man from the South' has clearly lost some bets with him in the past. Imagine one of these and write the story.

23 The pilot in 'Beware of the Dog' remembers the advice he received in England about what he should do if he is caught by the enemy. Write this advice as a speech by an officer to his pilots who are going to fly into battle.

24 Write a newspaper article about the disappearance of Christopher Mulholland or Gregory Temple in 'The Landlady'. Use information from the text and invent any other details that you need.

25 Write one of these conversations:

   a the conversation between Mr Boggis and the farmers when Mr Boggis returns to collect his commode in 'The Vicar's Pleasure'.

   b the conversation in which Claud first persuaded Bessie Organ to help him with his poaching in 'The Champion of the World'.

26 Write about Lexington's first impressions and experience of New York City when he arrives there in 'Pig'. How does the city compare with his home environment? How does he feel?

27 Imagine what happens before 'An African Story' begins. Who are Judson and the old man and why did they decide to work together on the farm? Write about their backgrounds and their first meeting.

BESTSELLING
PENGUIN READERS

AT LEVEL 6

Brave New World

The Chamber

Cry, the Beloved Country

Great Expectations

Kolymsky Heights

Memoirs of a Geisha

Misery

Oliver Twist

Presumed Innocent

The Remains of the Day

Saving Private Ryan

Snow Falling on Cedars